The Faber Book of Useful Verse

THE FABER BOOK OF
Useful Verse

Edited with an Introduction
SIMON BRETT

FABER AND FABER
London and Boston

First published in 1981
by Faber and Faber Limited
3 Queen Square London WC1N 3AU
Phototypeset by Western Printing Services Ltd, Bristol
Printed in Great Britain by
Redwood Burn Ltd, Trowbridge
All rights reserved

British Library Cataloguing in Publication Data

The Faber book of useful verse
1. Poetry—Collections
I. Brett, Simon, 1943
808.81   PN6101

ISBN 0-571-11781-3
ISBN 0-571-11782-1 Pbk

Contents

Chronological List of Writers		*page* 9
Introduction		19

Useful for:

1	Dates	24
2	Weather Forecasts	31
3	Farmers and Gardeners	36
4	Lovers (Male)	56
5	Lovers (Female)	63
6	Those Contemplating Matrimony	74
7	Those Contemplating Children	81
8	The Upbringing of Children	85
9	Medicine	105
10	Cooks	121
11	English	133
12	Aspiring Poets	150
13	History	158
14	Latin	170
15	The Sciences	174
16	Mathematics	186
17	Geography	192
18	Religious Knowledge	194
19	Financiers	201
20	Advertisement	203

CONTENTS

21 Gift-tags   *page* 218

22 Inscriptions in Books   229

23 Correspondence   235

24 Miscellaneous Occasions   245

25 All Circumstances   251

Acknowledgements   253

Chronological List of Writers

HESIOD (8th century BC)
49 From *Works and Days* (Book II)

NICOCHARES (c. 400 BC)
96 Hangover Cure

NICOPHON (c. 400 BC)
97 Beware of Figs

AMPHIS (4th century BC)
96 Hangover Cure

ARCHESTRATUS (4th century BC)
117 From *Gastrology*
119 Recipe from *The Deipnosophists of Athenaeus*

AXIONICUS (4th century BC)
119 Recipe from *The Deipnosophists of Athenaeus*

EUBULUS (4th century BC)
95 The Benefits and Abuse of Alcohol

SOTADES (4th century BC)
119 Recipe from *The Deipnosophists of Athenaeus*

PHILEMON (361–263 BC)
119 Recipe from *The Deipnosophists of Athenaeus*

ALEXIS (c. 350 BC)
96 Hangover Cure

NICANDER (2nd century BC)
119 Recipe from *The Deipnosophists of Athenaeus*

VIRGIL (70–19 BC)
11 How to Predict the Weather
17 The Care of Bees

OVID (43 BC–18 AD)
32 From the First Book of Ovid's *Art of Love*
41 From Ovid's Third Book of *The Art of Love*

MAYSTER BENET (15th century)
134 The Alphabet of Aristotle

SIR ANTHONY FITZHERBERT (1470–1538)
264 Memorial Verses for Travellers

RICHARD GRAFTON (?–1572)
1 The Months of the Year

THOMAS TUSSER (1524?–80)
15 From *A Hundreth Good Poyntes of Husbandry*

M. SAINT-MARTHE (Physician to Henry III of France) (fl. 1580)
66 Cravings during Pregnancy
67 Labour
70 Choosing a Wet-Nurse
100 Infant Diseases and Their Treatment

SIR PHILIP SIDNEY (1554–86)
145 Grammar-Rules

JOHN WILLIS (?–1628?)
265 Verses to be Repeated by an Attorney Leaving His Lodging to Wait upon Judges Riding the Circuits from One County to Another

ROBERT HERRICK (1591–1674)
29 A Charme, or an Allay for Love
36 To Women, to Hide Their Teeth, If They be Rotten or Rusty
63 Observation
236 A Ternarie of Littles, upon a Pipkin of Jellie Sent to a Lady
251 Useful for Book-Plates

THOMAS CAREW (1595–1640)
237 The Primrose

CLAUDE QUILLET (1602–61)
64 The Best Time for Conception

65 How to Conceive Boys
101 The Process of Conception

THOMAS BARKER (fl. 1651)
120 Methods of Cooking Trout
268 How to Catch Trout
269 Baits for Various Fish

MARGARET CAVENDISH, DUCHESS OF NEWCASTLE (1624–74)
177 What is Liquid

THOMAS SAFFOLD (?–1691)
212 Saffold's Cures

JOHN DRYDEN (1631–1700)
11 How to Predict the Weather (Virgil)
17 The Care of Bees (Virgil)
32 From the First Book of Ovid's *Art of Love*

WENTWORTH DILLON, EARL OF ROSCOMMON (1633–85)
155 From *An Essay on Translated Verse*

THOMAS FLATMAN (1635–88)
51 On Marriage

CHARLES SACKVILLE, EARL OF DORSET (1638–1706)
30 The Advice

SIR CHARLES SEDLEY (1639–1701)
31 Advice to the Old Beaux

JOHN CASE (fl. 1680–1700)
213 To Saffold's Customers
214 Over Case's Door
215 From One of Case's Pill-Boxes

JOHN SHEFFIELD, DUKE OF BUCKINGHAM AND NORMANBY
    (1648–1721)
154 On Writing for the Stage

SIR RICHARD BLACKMORE (1653–1729)
102 The Circulation of the Blood

JOSIAH CHORLEY (?–1719?)
201 From *A Metrical Index to the Bible*

WILLIAM WALSH (1663–1708)
53 Against Marriage to His Mistress

WILLIAM KING (1663–1712)
118 From *The Art of Cookery*
123 From *The Art of Making Puddings*

MATTHEW PRIOR (1664–1721)
40 Written in an Ovid

JONATHAN SWIFT (1667–1745)
124 Onyons
140 On the Vowels—a Riddle
216 Inscription for the Sign of 'The Jolly Barber' with a Razor in One Hand, and a Pot of Beer in the Other
255 A True and Faithful Inventory of the Goods Belonging to Dr Swift, Vicar of Laracor

WILLIAM CONGREVE (1670–1729)
41 From Ovid's Third Book of *The Art of Love*

ISAAC WATTS (1674–1748)
71 Love between Brothers and Sisters

WILLIAM SOMERVILLE (1675–1742)
37 Advice to the Ladies

JOHN PHILIPS (1676–1709)
21 Pruning
22 How to Catch Wasps

SAMUEL SHOWELL, JR. (fl. 1717)
252 An Item from the Scrapbooks of E. Wilson Dobbs

JOHN GAY (1685–1732)
38 Traditional Charm for Finding the Identity of One's True Love
121 A Receipt for Stewing Veal
238 To a Young Lady, with Some Lampreys

AARON HILL (1685–1750)
203 The Lord's Prayer in Verse

GEORGE SEWELL (1688?–1726)
64 The Best Time for Conception (Claude Quillet)
65 How to Conceive Boys (Claude Quillet)
101 The Process of Conception (Claude Quillet)

ALEXANDER POPE (1688–1744)
153 From *An Essay on Criticism*

PHILIP STANHOPE, EARL OF CHESTERFIELD (1694–1773)
42 Advice to a Lady in Autumn

MATTHEW GREEN (1696–1737)
103 In Praise of Water-Gruel

JOHN DYER (1699–1758)
18 How to Shear Sheep

ROBERT BARCLAY (1699–1760)
251 Useful for Book-Plates

DR GREENWOOD (18th century)
114 Epitaph

THOMAS COOKE (1703–56)
49 From Hesiod's *Works and Days* (Book II)

ROBERT DODSLEY (1703–64)
23 A Method of Preserving Hay from being Mow-Burnt, or
Taking Fire

SOAME JENYNS (1704–87)
34 and 43 From *The Art of Dancing*

HENRY FOX, LORD HOLLAND (1705–74)
244 With a China Chamberpot, to the Countess of Hills-
borough

NATHANIEL COTTON (1705–88)
55 Marriage

GEORGE LYTTELTON (1709–73)
239 To Miss Lucy F——, with a New Watch,

JOHN ARMSTRONG (1709–79)
104 The Advantages of Washing
105 The Dangers of Sexual Excess

JAMES GRAINGER (1721–66)
19 How to Fertilize Soil
20 How to Exterminate Rats

CHRISTOPHER SMART (1722–71)
24 How to Cure Hops and Prepare Them for Sale

WILL JACKETT (?–1789)
258 Extraordinary Will

WILLIAM MASON (1724–97)
26 How to Build a Ha-ha

JOHN CUNNINGHAM (1729–73)
240 Sent to Miss Bell H——, with a Pair of Buckles

JOHN SCOTT (1730–83)
25 How to Fertilize Soil

WILLIAM COWPER (1731–1800)
28 How to Grow Cucumbers

ERASMUS DARWIN (1731–1802)
27 The Protection of Plants
179 The Action of Electricity
180 The Action of Invisible Ink

RICHARD CUMBERLAND (1732–1811)
95 The Benefits and Abuse of Alcohol (*The Deipnosophists of Athenaeus*)

CHARLES BRANDLING (1733–1802)
246 To a Lady, with a Present of a Fan

ROBERT LLOYD (1733–64)
241 Sent to a Lady, with a Seal

JOHN COLLINS (1742–1808)
167 The Chapter of Kings

GAVIN WILSON (fl. 1779)
220 From the *Caledonian Mercury*

EDWARD JENNER (1749–1823)
12 Signs of Rain
242 Sent to a Patient, with the Present of a Couple of Ducks

THE HON. GEORGE NAPIER (1751–1804)
245 To a Lady, with a Compass

GEORGE HARDING (?–1816)
260 Reply to a Creditor

THOMAS CHATTERTON (1752–70)
186 The Copernican System

GEORGE CRABBE (1754–1832)
 59 Marriages

ROBERT BURNS (1759–96)
257 The Inventory

RICHARD PORSON (1759–1808)
174 On the Latin Gerunds

ISAAC D'ISRAELI (1766–1848)
117 From *Gastrology* (Archestratus)

JOHN HOOKHAM FRERE (1769–1846)
248 To a Lady, with a Present of a Walking-Stick .

SYDNEY SMITH (1771–1845)
125 Recipe for Salad

SAMUEL TAYLOR COLERIDGE (1772–1834)
152 Metrical Feet
191 A Mathematical Problem

JOHN JONES (1774–?)
247 To Lydia, with a Coloured Egg, on Easter Monday

WILLIAM HALL (fl. 1810)
222 An Auctioneer's Handbill

JAMES SMITH (1775–1839)
197 On the American Rivers

WALTER SAVAGE LANDOR (1775–1865)
262 To Alfred Tennyson

ADELAIDE O'KEEFFE (1776–1855)
 77 To George Pulling Buds
 80 Rather Too Good, Little Peggy!

ANNE TAYLOR (1782–1866)
79 Washing and Dressing

JANE TAYLOR (1783–1824)
78 The Disappointment

LEIGH HUNT (1784–1859)
168 The Royal Line

THOMAS LOVE PEACOCK (1785–1866)
259 A Letter from School

GEORGE GORDON, LORD BYRON (1788–1824)
243 Stanzas to a Lady, with the Poems of Camoëns
261 Epistle to Mr. Murray

RICHARD H. BARHAM (1788–1845)
263 Lines Left at Mr. Theodore Hook's House in June, 1834

SOLYMAN BROWN (1790–1865?)
107 The Value of Dentistry
108 Tartar
109 Caries
110 Artificial Teeth

JOHN CLARE (1793–1864)
39 From *The Shepherd's Calendar*

BENJAMIN HALL KENNEDY (1804–89)
5 The Roman Calendar
171 Memorial Lines on the Gender of Latin Substantives

THOMAS BAKER (?–1871)
182 Watt's Improvements to the Steam Engine
183 Means of Propulsion for Steam-Ships
184 The Electric Telegraph

HEINRICH HOFFMAN (1809–74)
81 The Story of Augustus who Would Not Have Any Soup

OLIVER WENDELL HOLMES (1809–94)
157 A Familiar Letter

EBENEZER COBHAM BREWER (1810–97)
6 The Signs of the Zodiac

WILLIAM MAKEPEACE THACKERAY (1811–63)
126 From *A Ballad of Bouillabaisse*

CHARLES DUKE YONGE (1812–91)
 96 Hangover Cures (*The Deipnosophists of Athenaeus*)
 97 Beware of Figs (*The Deipnosophists of Athenaeus*)
119 Recipes from *The Deipnosophists of Athenaeus*

LEVI ROCKWELL (fl. 1853)
225 From a Connecticut Newspaper

MATTHEW ARNOLD (1822–88)
158 A Caution to Poets

LEWIS CARROLL (1832–98)
 76 Rules and Regulations
185 Facts

PETER MINCK (fl. 1868)
228 Pain Paint

H. J. BYRON (1834–84)
 14 An Adage

W. S. GILBERT (1836–1911)
 35 From *The Yeomen of the Guard*

EDWARD B. GOODWIN (fl. 1875)
151 Principal British Writers
159 From *Roman History in Rhyme*
169 From *English History in Rhyme*

GERARD MANLEY HOPKINS (1844–89)
 94 Spring and Fall

G. P. LATHROP (fl. 1882)
249 A Feather's Weight

ROBERT LOUIS STEVENSON (1850–94)
 85 Whole Duty of Children

OWEN SEAMAN (1861–1936)
 44 Time's Revenges

LORD ALFRED DOUGLAS (1870–1945)
250 To ——, with an Ivory Hand-glass

HILAIRE BELLOC (1870–1953)
89 Henry King
90 Franklin Hyde

R. RHODES (fl. 1907)
231 A Prize-Winning Limerick

A. P. HERBERT (1890–1971)
7 Inst., Ult., and Prox.

DOROTHY PARKER (1893–1967)
45 Social Note
46 Unfortunate Coincidence
47 News Item

JUSTIN RICHARDSON (b. 1899)
2 Rhyme for Remembering How Many Nights There are
   in the Month
4 Rhyme for Remembering the Date of Easter

OGDEN NASH (1902–70)
60 The Perfect Husband
92 Reflection on Babies
93 Lines to be Embroidered on a Bib
131 Celery

GORDON PERRY (b. 1909)
176 Aids for Latin
198 The Great Lakes of Canada

WILLARD R. ESPY (b. 1910)
148 Singular Singulars, Peculiar Plurals
187 Gemini Jones

MICHAEL FLANDERS (1922–75)
190 First and Second Law

DONALD MONAT (fl. 1959)
194 Rhymed Mnemonic of the Forty Counties of England

TOM LEHRER (b. 1928)
188 The Elements
193 New Maths

Introduction

Groucho Marx once condemned as useless all poetry, except for the six-line verse which begins 'Thirty days hath September . . .', whose usefulness was obvious. Equally it could be argued that all poetry is in some way useful—even *Paradise Lost* is useful in justifying the ways of God to Men—and so could qualify for this anthology.

In making my selection, I have taken a middle course between these extremes. Since this is the first anthology of Useful Verse, I have had the luxury of making my own definitions.

In my starting point, I agree with Groucho Marx. 'Thirty days hath September . . .' is there, leading a large field of mnemonic and memorial verses. My search for these proved entertaining and, at times, frustrating. By their nature, many such verses belong to an oral rather than a written tradition and, though people remember snatches of them, it is sometimes difficult to home in on a complete version. And a lot of favourite mnemonics (for example, 'Richard Of York Gained Battles In Vain' for the colours of the spectrum, or the musical one, 'Every Good Boy Deserves Favour') are disqualified from selection by not being in verse. But many remain that do fit the brief and are in the book. I am sure that many others have escaped my net. There are probably mnemonic rhymes for every profession and discipline and I hope, in time, to track them down.

If I had stuck rigidly to the Groucho Marx principle of selection, this would be a very short book; and if I had not strayed beyond mnemonics, it would be a very unvaried one. So I have extended the field of Usefulness to include verse which is instructive or functional. Under the banner of 'instructive' I have enlisted works whose application is physical or specific, rather than just moral. Maybe there is room in the world for an anthology of morally didactic verse, but this is not it.

'Useful', I discovered early in my researches, is a word of such elastic definition that it needs constant qualification. If I did not say what a verse was useful *for*, my reasons for its selection might remain obscure. This realization also gave me the key to a method of categorizing the items. By breaking them down into sections ('Useful for Cooks', 'Useful for History', etc.), I had not only found a way of signposting the selection, but also avoided the chronological straitjacket which threatens all anthologists.

I make no apology for the large amount of material from the eighteenth century, because that was the Golden Age of Useful Verse. Though their worst excesses were painfully artificial, at their best eighteenth-century poets demonstrated the supreme flexibility of blank verse and heroic couplets *on any subject*. There was good poetry and bad poetry, but there was not yet the distinction, on the grounds of subject matter, between 'Poetry' on the one hand and, on the other, the pejorative, 'Verse'. It was the Romantic Movement (which has a lot to answer for in many ways) which changed all that.

Wordsworth's much-quoted—and at the time much-derided—Preface to the second edition of the *Lyrical Ballads* (1800) laid down certain principles which have retrospectively been identified with Romantic Poetry. By stressing the need for simple language ('What is a poet? To whom does he address himself? And what language is to be expected of him?—He is a man speaking to men'), Wordsworth showed up the mannerisms of eighteenth-century verse, the elaborate personifications and verbiage which distanced the poet's emotion from the reader; but the new emphasis ('For all good poetry is the spontaneous overflow of powerful feelings: and though this be true, Poems to which any value can be attached were never produced on any variety of subjects but by a man who, being possessed of more than usual organic sensibility, had also thought long and deeply') brought with it new restrictions in subject matter. Poetry now sought a direct emotional reaction; it might teach the reader how to respond to the passions of life, it might teach him tempestuous and inexact ideas of revolution, but it no longer demeaned itself by teaching him mere facts.

In the eighteenth century, by contrast, everything was the poet's province. Poetry was a true alternative to prose, and sometimes offered a tidier form of packaging for information. It was the age of the *Art of* . . . Translated from the classics, or based on classical models, there was room for an *Art of* . . . everything. Some were ridiculously inflated, some were deliberately humorous, but all contained a good volume of Useful information. The aim was elegance of expression, whatever the subject matter. The principle was well laid out by William Mason in his poem, *The English Garden* (1772–82), as he shaped up to the task of describing how to build a ha-ha:

> Ingrateful sure,
> When such the theme, becomes the poet's task:
> Yet must he try, by modulation meet
> Of varied cadence, and selected phrase,
> Exact yet free, without inflation bold,
> To dignify that theme, must try to form
> Such magic sympathy of sense with sound
> As pictures all it sings; while grace awakes
> At each blest touch, and, on the lowliest things,
> Scatters her rainbow hues.

It may be difficult, but there is no questioning the fact that the poet *must* try.

Half a century later such an attitude had become something to apologize for. When, in 1833, Solyman Brown, an American, wrote *Dentologia: A Poem on the Diseases of the Teeth, and their Proper Remedies*, he knew he was producing an oddity:

> Full well I know 'tis difficult to chime
> The laws of science with the rules of rhyme;
> Plain vulgar prose, my subject seems to claim,
> Did not ambition prompt the higher aim,
> The nobler pride, by more laborious care,
> To speak in numbers that shall please the fair.

The Romantic Movement had intervened, and Useful Poetry never recovered; thereafter, if it was Useful, it was, almost by definition, Verse. Poetry, except for the purely narrative, now had an emotional rather than an instructive purpose, and Useful Verse became the province of schoolmasters and humorists.

Of course, humour had always been there. Many of the eighteenth-century poets were deliberately writing in a mock-epic style, but this enhanced rather than diminished the usefulness of the information that they put across. Some, of course, were totally straight-faced—any humour in James Grainger's *The Sugar-Cane* is unintentional—but John Philips in *Cyder* or Christopher Smart in *The Hop-Garden* had their tongues firmly in the area of their cheeks, as is obvious from a reading of their works.

A danger that might threaten a selection of Useful Verse is that it could become a selection of Bad Verse. But, though some of the mnemonics are a little shaky on euphony and scansion, that is not the intention of this anthology. There may be Five Stuffed Owls in the 'Useful for Advertisement' section, but the book offers no challenge to *The Stuffed Owl*, that definitive selection of Bad Verse.

A point that struck me repeatedly in my researches was how different the selection might have been even fifty years ago, when classical education was much more the norm than it is now. The great classical authors provided models of Useful Verse, and many mnemonics were formulated to help in the learning of Latin and Greek. Latin verse was sufficiently familiar for the fitting of a miscellaneous list into hexameters to be reckoned a useful aid to memory—an assumption which could no longer be made with any confidence. Recognizing the decline of classical knowledge, I have limited the number of Latin mnemonics and handy hexameters. But no doubt, as some subjects drop off school curricula, the ones that replace them develop their own *aides-mémoire*. I look forward to discovering rhyming mnemonics for sociology, computer programming and micro-electronics.

A selection of this sort owes a huge debt to the long tradition of anthologists, from Athenaeus onwards, and to the work of many scholars, whose books I have consulted. Those volumes on which my reliance has been sufficient to merit individual recognition must include Chalmers' *The English Poets* (1810), Dodsley's *Collection of Poems* (1748), Sampson's *History of Advertising* (1874) and that inestimable source of knowledge, the collected editions of *Notes and Queries*. And I am most grateful to the staff and shelves of the London Library and the British Library.

There are also individuals without whose help this book would not have appeared in its present form, and to whom I would like to extend my gratitude: first, Adam Roberts, whose idea the anthology was; and then, for pointing me in Useful directions, the following: Frank Armstrong, Eileen G. Batts, Virginia Bell, Trevor Emmott, Chris Hutton, Chris Miller, Frank Muir, Gordon Perry, the people who kindly answered my appeal in the Personal columns of *The Times*, and all the others who obligingly racked their brains for half-forgotten rhymes from their schooldays.

The process of selection has been an enormously enjoyable one for me, and I hope that enjoyment communicates itself to the reader. To conclude, a few lines from Matthew Prior's *Alma, or the Progress of the Mind*:

> First, poets, all the world agrees,
> Write half to profit, half to please.
> Matter and figure they produce;
> For garnish this, and that for use;
> And, in the structure of their feasts,
> They seek to feed and please their guests.

I hope that this anthology serves the two purposes of feeding and pleasing.

SIMON BRETT

1 Useful for Dates

1 The Months of the Year

Thirty days hath September,
April, June, and November,
February eight-and-twenty all alone
And all the rest have thirty-one,
Unless that Leap Year doth
   combine
And give to February twenty-nine.

ANON

Thirty days hath November,
April, June, and September,
February hath twenty-eight alone,
And all the rest have thirty-one.

RICHARD GRAFTON (?–1572)

Fourth, eleventh, ninth, and sixth,
Thirty days to each affix;
Every other thirty-one,
Except the second month alone.

ANON

2 Rhyme for Remembering How Many Nights There are in the Month

Thirty-*one* nights hath December,
Plus six others we remember—
Jan., July, Aug., May, Mar., Oct.
The rest to thirty nights are docked,
Save Feb., which twenty-nine hath clear,
And twenty-eight each un-leap year.

JUSTIN RICHARDSON (b. 1899)

3 Memorial Verses, Adapted to the Gregorian Account, or New Style

To Know if it be Leap Year

Leap year is given, when four will divide
The cent'ries complete, or odd years beside.

Example for 1752.

4)<u>52</u>(0, Leap Year
13

Example for 1800.

4)<u>18</u>(2, not Leap Year
4

To find the Dominical Letter★

Divide the cent'ries by four; and twice what does remain,
Take from six; and then add to the number you gain
The odd years and their fourth; which, dividing by seven,
What is left take from seven, and the letter is given.

Example for 1752.

4)17(1
  —2
4<u> </u>
  2
  <u>6</u>
  4
  52
  13
  <u>7</u>
7)<u>69</u>(6
  9 1 = A

★The Dominical Letter, or Sunday Letter, is one of the first seven of the alphabet. If 1 January is a Sunday, the letter is A, if a Monday B, if a Tuesday C, and so on.

By the Dominical Letter, to find on what day of the week any day of the month will fall throughout the year

At Dover dwells George Brown, Esquire,
Good Christopher Finch, and David Frier.

Example for 9 May 1752.
(A being the Dominical Letter)
  1 May = B = Monday

  $\frac{7}{8}$ = Monday

  $\frac{1}{9}$ = Tuesday

To find the Golden Number,* Cycle of the Sun,† and Roman Indiction‡

When, one, nine, three, to the year have added been,
Divide by nineteen, twenty-eight, fifteen:
By what remains each cycle's year is seen.

Examples for 1752.

1752	1752
1	9
19)1753(92	28)1761(62
43	81
5 = G.No.	25 = Cy.S.

*The Golden Number (or 'Prime') is the number of the year on the Metonic Cycle (a 19-year cycle at the end of which the new moons fall on the same days of the year). It is therefore a number between 1 and 19.

†The Cycle of the Sun is a 28-year period, at the end of which the days of the month fall on the same days of the week as they did at the beginning.

‡The Roman Indiction was a fiscal period of 15 years, at the beginning of which Roman property tax was reassessed. It was reckoned from 1 September 312 AD.

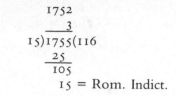

$$15 = \text{Rom. Indict.}$$

A general rule for the Epact★

Let the cent'ries by four be divided; and then
What remains multiplied by the number seventeen;
Forty-three times the quotient, and eighty-six more
Add to that; and dividing by five and a score;
From eleven times the prime, subtract the last quote,
Which, rejecting the thirties, gives th'epact you sought.

Example for 1752.

```
4)17( 1                    G. No. =  5
   17                                11
  ___                                55
   4                                 11
  43                           30)44(1
  172                          14 = Epact.
   86
   17
25)275(1
```

To find Easter Limit, or the day of the Paschal Full Moon, from March 1, inclusive

Add six to the epact, reject three times ten,
What's left take from fifty, the limit you gain:
Which, if fifty, one less you must make it, and even
When forty-nine too, if prime's more than eleven.

★The Epact is the excess of the solar year (365 days) over the lunar year (354 days). It is the number of days from the last new moon of the old year to the first of the January of the new year.

[27]

Example
Epact = 14
       6
      ──
      20
      50
      ──
      30 = Limit.

To find Easter Day

If the letter and four from the limit you take,
And what's left from next number which sevens will make;
Adding then to the limit what last does remain,
You the days from St. David's* to Easter obtain.

Example.
Limit = 30   A = 1
        5   4
       ──   ──
       25   5
       28 = next sevens
       ──
        3
       30 = Limit
       ──
       33 Days
       31 = March
       ──
     April 2 Easter Day

ANON

From an 1861 reprint of Grey's *Memoria Technica*

*St David's Day is 1 March.

4 Rhyme for Remembering the Date of Easter

No need for confusion if we but recall
That Easter on the first Sunday after the full moon
  following the vernal equinox doth fall.
                    JUSTIN RICHARDSON (b. 1899)

5 The Roman Calendar

March, May, July, October; these are they
Make Nones the 7th, Ides the 15th day.
          BENJAMIN HALL KENNEDY (1804–89)
                  From *The Revised Latin Primer*

6 The Signs of the Zodiac

Our vernal signs the RAM begins,
Then comes the BULL, in May the TWINS;
The CRAB in June, next LEO shines,
And VIRGO ends the northern signs.
The BALANCE brings autumnal fruits,
The SCORPION stings, the ARCHER shoots;
December's GOAT brings wintry blast,
AQUARIUS rain, the FISH comes last.
          EBENEZER COBHAM BREWER (1810–97)

7 Inst., Ult., and Prox.

Write a love-lyric about the months of Inst. Ult., and Prox.

Answer

I heard the happy lark exult,
Too soon, for it was early ult.;
And now the land with rain is rinsed—
Ah, mournful is the month of inst.;
Love, like a lizard in the rocks,
Is hungry for the suns of prox.

Boy Cupid with his catapult
Could find but sorry sport in ult.;
But through the woods, with bluebells chintzed,
My lady comes to me in inst.:
And O may Cupid speed the clocks,
For she will marry me in prox!

A. P. HERBERT (1890–1971)
From *What A Word!*

8 Proverbial Weather Rhymes

The South wind brings wet weather;
The North wind wet and cold together;
The West wind brings us rain;
The East wind blows it back again.

Spring is showery, flowery, bowery;
Summer: hoppy, croppy, poppy;
Autumn: slippy, drippy, nippy;
Winter: breezy, sneezy, freezy.

When the ash is before the oak,
We are sure to have a soak.
When the oak's before the ash,
We shall only have a splash.

When the wind is in the East,
It's neither good for man nor beast,
When the wind is in the North,
The skilful fisher goes not forth.
When the wind is in the South,
It blows the bait in the fish's mouth.
When the wind is in the West,
Then it is at its very best.

9 Proverbially Useful Dates for Weathermen

If St Paul* be fair and clear,
Then betides a happy year.

If Candlemas Day† be fair and bright,
Winter will have another flight;
If on Candlemas Day it be shower and rain,
Winter is gone and will not come again.

Rain on Good Friday and Easter Day,
A good year for grass, and a bad year for hay.

If the First of July be rainy weather,
It will rain, more or less, for four weeks together.

If the twenty-fourth of August be fair and clear,
Then hope for a prosperous autumn that year.

10 Proverbially Useful for Weather Forecasts

When clouds appear like rocks and towers,
The earth's refreshed by frequent showers.

Mackerel sky, mackerel sky,
Not long wet and not long dry.

*25 January   †2 February

[32]

When black snails cross your path,
Black clouds much moisture hath.

Evening red and morning grey,
Are the sure signs of a fine day.

Red sky in the morning,
Shepherd's warning.
Red sky at night,
Shepherd's delight.

*(Anonymous 20th-century addition
to above:*

Sky in red mist,
Shepherd pissed.)

11 How to Predict the Weather

Observe the daily circle of the sun,
And the short year of each revolving moon:
By them thou shalt foresee the following day,
Nor shall a starry night thy hopes betray.
When first the moon appears, if then she shrouds
Her silver crescent tipped with sable clouds,
Conclude she bodes a tempest on the main,
And brews for fields impetuous floods of rain.
Or, if her face with fiery flushing glow,
Expect the rattling winds aloft to blow.
But, four nights old (for that's the surest sign),
With sharpened horns if glorious then she shine,

Next day, nor only that, but all the moon,
'Till her revolving race be wholly run,
Are void of tempests, both by land and sea,
And sailors in the port their promised vow shall pay.

* * *

But, more than all, the setting sun survey,
When down the steep of heaven he drives the day:
For oft we find him finishing his race,
With various colours erring on his face.
If fiery red his glowing globe descends,
High winds and furious tempests he portends:
But, if his cheeks are swoln with livid blue,
He bodes wet weather by his water hue:
If dusky spots are varied on his brow,
And, streaked with red, a troubled colour show;
That sullen mixture shall at once declare
Winds, rain, and storms, and elemental war.

VIRGIL (70–19 BC)
From *Georgics* (Book I)
Translated by JOHN DRYDEN (1631–1700)

12 Signs of Rain

*(An Excuse for not joining a Friend in an
Excursion)*

The hollow winds begin to blow,
The clouds look black, the glass is low,
The soot falls down, the spaniels sleep,
The spiders from their cobwebs peep,
Last night the sun went pale to bed,
The moon in halos hid her head;
The boding shepherd heaves a sigh,
For, see, a rainbow spans the sky.
The walls are damp, the ditches smell,
Closed is the pink-eyed pimpernell.

[34]

Hark! how the chairs and tables crack,
Old Betty's joints are on the rack;
Loud quack the ducks, the peacocks cry,
The distant hills are looking nigh.
How restless are the snorting swine,
The busy flies disturb the kine;
Low o'er the grass the swallow wings;
The cricket, too, how sharp he sings.
Puss on the hearth, with velvet paws,
Sits, wiping o'er his whisker'd jaws.
Through the clear stream the fishes rise,
And nimbly catch th'incautious flies;
The glowworms, numerous and bright,
Illumed the dewy dell last night.
At dusk the squalid toad was seen,
Hopping and crawling o'er the green;
The whirling wind the dust obeys,
And in the rapid eddy plays;
The frog has changed his yellow vest,
And in a russet coat is drest.
Though June, the air is cold and still;
The yellow blackbird's voice is shrill.
My dog, so alter'd in his taste,
Quits mutton bones, on grass to feast;
And see, yon rooks, how odd their flight,
They imitate the gliding kite,
And seem precipitate to fall—
As if they felt the piercing ball.
'Twill surely rain, I see with sorrow;
Our jaunt must be put off to-morrow.

DR EDWARD JENNER (1749–1823)

3 Useful for Farmers and Gardeners

13 Proverbial Advice for the Farmer

Upon St David's Day,★
Put oats and barley in the clay.

St Benedick,†
Sow thy pease or keep them in the rick.

A cold April
The barn doth fill.

A cold May and a windy
Makes a full barn and a findy.‡

Shear your sheep in May,
And shear them all away.

Look at your corn in May,
And you'll come weeping away;
Look at the same in June,
And you'll come home to another tune.

A dripping June
Brings all things in tune.

★1 March   †21 March   ‡plentiful

[36]

Dry August and warm
Doth harvest no harm.

Sow thin,
and mow thin.

This rule in gardening ne'er forget,
To sow dry and set wet.

Sow beans in the mud,
And they'll grow like mud.

Barley straw's good fodder
When the cow gives water.

Cut thistles in May,
They grow in a day;
Cut them in June,
That is too soon;
Cut them in July,
Then they will die.

14 An Adage

The gardener's rule applies to youth and age:
When young 'sow wild oats', but when old, grow sage.

H. J. BYRON (1834–84)

15 *From* A Hundreth Good Poyntes of Husbandry

August

9   When harvest is done all thing placed and set,
for saultfishe and herring then laie for to get:
The byeng of them, comming first unto rode,
shal pay for thy charges thou spendest abrode.

September

20   Threshe sede and goe fanne, for the plough may not
       lye,
September doth bid to be sowing of rye:
The redges well harrowde or euer thou strike,
is one poynt of husbandry rye land do like.

October

25   The rye in the ground while September doth last:
October for wheate sowing, calleth as fast.
What euer it cost thee what euer thou geue,
haue done sowing wheate before halowmas eve.

November

33   For Easter at Martilmas hange up a biefe:
for pease fed and stall fed, play pickpurse the thiefe.
With that and fat bakon, till grasse biefe come in:
thy folke shall loke cherely when others loke thin.

December

40   Serue first out thy rie strawe then wheate & then pease,
     then otestrawe then barley, then hay if you please.
     But serue them with haye while thy straw stoouer last,
     they loue no more strawe they had rather to fast.

Christmas

42   Get iuye and hull, woman deck up thyne house:
     and take this same brawne, for to seeth and to souse.
     Prouide us good chere, for thou knowst the old guise:
     olde customes, that good be, let no man dispise.

43   At Christmas be mery, and thanke god of all:
     and feast thy pore neighbours, the great with the small.
     yea al the yere long haue an eie to the poore:
     and god shall sende luck, to kepe open thy doore.

January

52   Thy coltes for the sadle geld yong to be light:
     for cart doe not so if thou iudgest a right.
     Nor geld not, but when they be lusty and fat:
     for there is a point to be learned in that.

Februarij

62   In Feuerell rest not for taking thine ease:
     get into the grounde with thy beanes and thy pease.
     Sow peason betimes and betimes they will come:
     the sooner the better they fill up a rome.

[39]

Marche

70 In Marche sow thy barley thy londe not to colde:
the drier the better a hundreth times tolde.
That tilthe harrowde finely, set sede time an ende:
and praise and pray God a good haruest to sende.

A Digression from Husbandrie: to a poynt or two of Huswifrie.

Now here I think nedeful a pawse for to make;
to treate of some paines a good huswife must take.
For huswifes must husband as wel as the man:
or farewel thy husbandrie do what thou can.

In Marche and in Aprill from morning to night:
in sowing and setting good huswiues delight.
To haue in their garden or some other plot:
to trim up their house and to furnish their pot.

Haue millons at Mihelmas, parsneps in lent:
in June, buttred beanes, saueth fish to be spent.
With those and good pottage inough hauing than:
thou winnest the heart of thy laboring man.

April

From Aprill begin til saint Andrew be past:
so long with good huswiues their dairies doe last.
Good milche bease and pasture, good husbandes
    prouide:
good husewiues know best all the rest how to guide.

[40]

May

78 In May at the furdest, twy fallow thy lande:
much drougth may cause after, thy plough els to
stande.
That tilth being done, thou hast passed the wurste:
then after, who plowgheth, plowgh thou with the
furste.

June

81 In June washe thy shepe, where the water doth runne:
and kepe them from dust, but not kepe them from
sunne.
Then share them and spare not, at two daies anende:
the sooner the better their bodies amende.

Julii

97 Reape well, scatter not, gather cleane that is shorne:
binde fast, shock a pase, pay the tenth of thy corne.
Lode salfe, carry home, lose no time, being faier:
golfe iust, in the barne, it is out of dispaier.

99 Then welcome thy haruest folke, seruantes and all:
with mirth and good chere, let them furnish thine hall.
The haruest lorde nightly, must geue thee a song:
fill him then the blacke boll, or els he hath wrong.

100 Thy haruest thus ended, in myrth and in ioye:
please euery one gently, man woman and boye.
Thus doing, with alway, such helpe as they can:
thou winnest the name, of a right husband man.

Finis

Nowe thinke upon god, let thy tonge neuer cease:
from thanking of him, for his myghty encrease.
Accept my good wil, finde no fault tyll thou trye:
the better thou thryuest, the gladder am I.

THOMAS TUSSER (1524?–80)

16 Ad Tusserum

Tusser, they tell me when thou wert alive,
Thou teaching thrift, thy self couldst never thrive;
So like the whetstone many men are wont
To sharpen others when themselves are blunt.

ANON

17 The Care of Bees

Now, when thou hast decreed to seize their stores,
And by prerogative to break their doors,
With sprinkled water first the city choke,
And then pursue the citizens with smoke.
Two honey-harvests fall in every year:
First, when the pleasing Pleiades appear,
And, springing upward, spurn the briny seas:
Again, when their affrighted choir surveys
The watery Scorpion mend his pace behind,
With a black train of storms, and winter wind,
They plunge into the deep, and safe protection find.
Prone to revenge, the bees, a wrathful race,
When once provoked, assault the aggressor's face,

[42]

And through the purple veins a passage find;
There fix their stings, and leave their souls behind.

VIRGIL (70–19 BC)
From *Georgics* (Book IV)
Translated by JOHN DRYDEN (1631–1700)

18 How to Shear Sheep

Now, jolly Swains! the harvest of your cares
Prepare to reap, and seek the sounding caves
Of high Brigantium, where, by ruddy flames,
Vulcan's strong sons, with nervous arm, around
The steady anvil and the glaring mass
Clatter their heavy hammers down by turns,
Flatt'ning the steel: from their rough hands receive
The sharpen'd instrument that from the flock
Severs the Fleece. If verdant elder spreads
Her silver flow'rs; if humble daisies yield
To yellow crow-foot, and luxuriant grass,
Gay shearing-time approaches. First, howe'er,
Drive to the double fold, upon the brim
Of a clear river, gently drive the flock,
And plunge them one by one into the flood:
Plung'd in the flood, not long the struggler sinks,
With his white flakes that glisten thro' the tide;
The sturdy rustic, in the middle wave,
Awaits to seize him rising; one arm bears
His lifted head above the limpid stream,
While the full clammy Fleece the other laves
Around, laborious, with repeated toil;
And then resigns him to the sunny bank,
Where, bleating loud, he shakes his dripping locks.
    Shear them the fourth or fifth return of morn,
Lest touch of busy fly-blows wound their skin.
Thy peaceful subjects without murmur yield
Their yearly tribute: 'tis the prudent part

To cherish and be gentle, while ye strip
The downy vesture from their tender sides.
Press not too close; with caution turn the points,
And from the head in regular rounds proceed;
But speedy, when he chance to wound, with tar
Prevent the wingy swarm and scorching heat.

JOHN DYER (1699–1758)
From *The Fleece* (Book II)

19 How to Fertilize Soil

Of composts shall the Muse descend to sing,
Nor soil her heavenly plumes? The sacred Muse
Nought sordid deems, but what is base; nought fair
Unless true Virtue stamp it with her seal.
Then, planter, wouldst thou double thine estate;
Never, ah never, be asham'd to tread
Thy dung-heaps, where the refuse of thy mills,
With all the ashes, all thy coppers yield,
With weeds, mould, dung, and stale, a compost form,
Of force to fertilize the poorest soil.

JAMES GRAINGER (1721–66)

20 How to Exterminate Rats

Nor with less waste the whisker'd vermin race,
A countless clan, despoil the low-land cane.
　These to destroy, while commerce hoists the sail,
Loose rocks abound, or tangling bushes bloom,
What planter knows?—Yet prudence may reduce.
Encourage then the breed of savage cats,
Nor kill the winding snake, thy foes they eat.
Thus, on the mangrove-banks of Guayaquil,

[44]

Child of the rocky desert, sea-like stream,
With studious care, the American preserves
The gallinazo, else that sea-like stream
(Whence Traffic pours her bounties on mankind)
Dread alligators would alone possess.
Thy foes, the teeth-fil'd Ibbos also love;
Nor thou their wayward appetite restrain.
    Some place decoys, nor will they not avail,
Replete with roasted crabs, in every grove
These fell marauders gnaw; and pay their slaves
Some small reward for every captive foe.
So practise Gallia's sons; but Britons trust
In other wiles; and surer their success.
    With Misnian arsenic, deleterious bane,
Pound up the ripe cassada's well-rasp'd root,
And form in pellets; these profusely spread
Round the cane-groves, where sculk the vermin breed:
They, greedy, and unweeting of the bait,
Crowd to the inviting cates, and swift devour
Their palatable death; for soon they seek
The neighbouring spring; and drink, and swell, and die.

JAMES GRAINGER (1721–66)
19 and 20 from *The Sugar-Cane* (Books I and II)

21 Pruning

                    Let the arched knife
Well sharpen'd now assail the spreading shades
Of vegetables, and their thirsty limbs
Dissever: for the genial moisture, due
To apples, otherwise mispends itself
In barren twigs, and for th'expected crop,
Nought but vain shoots, and empty leaves abound.
    When swelling buds their odorous foliage shed,
And gently harden into fruit, the wise
Spare not the little offsprings, if they grow

[45]

Redundant; but the thronging clusters thin
By kind avulsion: else the starveling brood,
Void of sufficient sustenance, will yield
A slender autumn; which the niggard soul
Too late shall weep, and curse his thrifty hand,
That would not timely ease the ponderous boughs.

JOHN PHILIPS (1676–1709)

22 How to Catch Wasps

Myriads of wasps now also clustering hang,
And drain a spurious honey from thy groves,
Their winter food; though oft repuls'd, again
They rally, undismay'd; but fraud with ease
Ensnares the noisome swarms; let every bough
Bear frequent vials, pregnant with the dregs
Of Moyle, or Mum, or Treacle's viscous juice;
They, by th'alluring odour drawn, in haste
Fly to the dulcet cates, and crowding sip
Their palatable bane; joyful thou'lt see
The clammy surface all o'erstrown with tribes
Of greedy insects, that with fruitless toil
Flap filmy pennons oft, to extricate
Their feet, in liquid shackles bound, till death
Bereave them of their worthless souls: such doom
Waits luxury, and lawless love of gain!

JOHN PHILIPS (1676–1709)
21 and 22 from *Cyder* (Book I)

23 A Method of Preserving Hay from Being Mow-Burnt, or Taking Fire

But do the threat'ning clouds precipitate
Thy work, and hurry to the field thy team,
Ere the Sun's heat, or penetrating wind,
Hath drawn its moisture from the fading grass?
Or hath the burning shower thy labours drench'd
With sudden inundation? Ah, with care
Accumulate thy load, or in the mow,
Or on the rising rick. The smother'd damps,
Fermenting, glow within; and latent sparks
At length engender'd, kindle by degrees,
Till, wide and wider spreading, they admit
The fatal blast, which instantly consumes,
In flames resistless, thy collected store.
This dire disaster to avoid, prepare
A hollow basket, or the concave round
Of some capacious vessel; to its sides
Affix a triple cord: then let the swains,
Full in the centre of thy purpos'd heap,
Place the obtrusive barrier; rising still
As they advance, by its united bands,
The wide machine. Thus leaving in its midst
An empty space, the coolling air draws in,
And from the flame, or from offensive taints
Pernicious to thy cattle, saves their food.

ROBERT DODSLEY (1703–64)
From *Agriculture* (Canto III)

24 How to Cure Hops and Prepare Them for Sale

Thus much be sung of picking—next succeeds
Th'important care of curing—Quit the field,
And at the kiln th'instructive muse attend.
    On your hair-cloth eight inches deep, nor more,
Let the green hops lie lightly; next expand
The smoothest surface with the toothy rake.
Thus far is just above; but more it boots
That charcoal flames burn equally below,
The charcoal flames, which from thy corded wood,
Or antiquated poles, with wond'rous skill,
The sable priests of Vulcan shall prepare.
Constant and moderate let the heat ascend;
Which to effect, there are, who with success
Place in the kiln the ventilating fan.
Hail, learned, useful man! whose head and heart
Conspire to make us happy, deign t'accept
One honest verse; and if thy industry
Has serv'd the hopland cause, the muse forebodes,
This sole invention, both in use and fame
The mystic fan of Bacchus shall exceed.
    When the fourth hour expires, with careful hand
The half-baked hops turn over. Soon as time
Has well exhausted twice two glasses more,
They'll leap and crackle with their bursting seeds,
For use domestic, or for sale mature.
    There are, who in the choice of cloth t' enfold
Their wealthy crop, the viler, coarser sort,
With prodigal oeconomy prefer:
All that is good is cheap, all dear that's base.
Besides the planter shou'd a bait prepare,
T'intrap the chapman's notice, and divert
Shrewd observation from her busy pry.
    When in the bag thy hops the rustic treads,
Let him wear heel-less sandals; nor presume
Their fragrancy barefooted to defile:

Such filthy ways for slaves in Malaga
Leave we to practise—whence I've oft seen,
When beautiful Dorinda's iv'ry hand
Has built the pastry-fabric (food divine
For Christmas gambols and the hour of mirth)
As the dry'd foreign fruit, with piercing eye,
She cull'd suspicious—lo! she starts, she frowns
With indignation at a negro's nail.

CHRISTOPHER SMART (1722–71)
From The Hop-Garden

25 How to Fertilize Soil

First

In vacant corners, on the hamlet waste,
The ample dunghill's steaming heap be plac'd;
There many a month fermenting to remain,
Ere thy slow team disperse it o'er the plain.

Second

The prudent farmer all manure provides,
The mire of roads, the mould of hedge-row sides;
For him their mud the stagnant ponds supply;
For him their soil, the stable and the sty.

Third

For this the swain, on Kennet's winding shore,
Digs sulphurous peat along the sable moor;
For this, where ocean bounds the stormy strand,
They fetch dank sea-weed to the neighb'ring land.

First

Who barren heaths to tillage means to turn,
Must, ere he plough, the greensward pare and burn;
Where rise the smoking hillocks o'er the field,
The saline ashes useful compost yield.

Second

Where sedge or rushes rise on spongy soils,
Or rampant moss th'impoverish'd herbage spoils,
Corrosive soot with lib'ral hand bestow;
Th'improving pasture soon its use will show.

Third

Hertfordian swains on airy hills explore
The chalk's white vein, a fertilizing store;
This from deep pits in copious baskets drawn,
Amends alike the arable and lawn.

JOHN SCOTT (1730–83)
From *Amoebaean Eclogues* (Eclogue II: 'Rural
Business; or, the Agriculturalists')

26 How to Build a Ha-ha

Since, then, constrain'd, we must expel the flock
From where our saplings rise, our flow'rets bloom,
The song shall teach, in clear preceptive notes,
How best to frame the fence, and best to hide
All its foreseen defects; defective still,
Tho'hid with happiest art. Ingrateful sure,

When such the theme, becomes the poet's task:
Yet must he try, by modulation meet
Of varied cadence, and selected phrase,
Exact yet free, without inflation bold,
To dignify that theme, must try to form
Such magic sympathy of sense with sound
As pictures all it sings; while grace awakes
At each blest touch, and, on the lowliest things,
Scatters her rainbow hues. The first and best
Is that, which, sinking from our eye, divides,
Yet seems not to divide the shaven lawn,
And parts it from the pasture; for if there
Sheep feed, or dappled deer, their wandering teeth
Will, smoothly as the scythe, the herbage shave,
And leave a kindred verdure. This to keep
Heed that thy labourer scoop the trench with care;
For some there are who give their spade repose,
When broad enough the perpendicular sides
Divide, and deep descend. To form perchance
Some needful drain, such labour may suffice,
Yet not for beauty: here thy range of wall
Must lift its height erect, and o'er its head
A verdant veil of swelling turf expand,
While smoothly from its base with gradual ease
The pasture meets its level, at that point
Which best deludes our eye, and best conceals
Thy lawn's brief limit. Down so smooth a slope
The fleecy foragers will gladly browse;
The velvet herbage free from weeds obscene
Shall spread its equal carpet, and the trench
Be pasture to its base. Thus form thy fence
Of stone, for stone alone, and pil'd on high,
Best curbs the nimble deer, that love to range
Unlimited; but where tame heifers feed,
Or innocent sheep, an humbler mound will serve
Unlin'd with stone, and but a green-sward trench.
Here midway down, upon the nearer bank
Plant thy thick rows of thorns, and to defend
Their infant shoots, beneath, on oaken stakes,

[51]

Extend a rail of elm, securely arm'd
With spiculated pailing, in such sort
As, round some citadel, the engineer
Directs his sharp stoccade.

WILLIAM MASON (1724–97)
From *The English Garden*

27 The Protection of Plants

'Sylphs! on each Oak-bud wound the wormy galls,
With pigmy spears, or crush the venom'd balls;
Fright the green Locust from his foamy bed,
Unweave the Caterpillar's gluey thread;
Chase the fierce Earwig, scare the bloated Toad,
Arrest the Snail upon his slimy road;
Arm with sharp thorns the Sweet-brier's tender wood,
And dash the Cynips from her damask bud;
Steep in ambrosial dews the Woodbine's bells,
And drive the Night-moth from her honey'd cells.
So where the Humming-bird in Chili's bowers
On murmuring pinions robs the pendent flowers;
Seeks, where fine pores their dulcet balm distill,
And sucks the treasure with proboscis-bill;
Fair CYPREPEDIA* with successful guile
Knits her smooth brow, extinguishes her smile;
A Spider's bloated paunch and jointed arms
Hide her fine form, and mask her blushing charms;
In ambush sly the mimic warrior lies,
And on quick wing the panting plunderer flies.

'Shield the young Harvest from devouring blight,
The Smut's dark poison, and the Mildew white;
Deep-rooted Mould, and Ergot's horn uncouth,
And break the Canker's desolating tooth.

*A South American plant.

[52]

First in one point the festering wound confin'd
Mines unperceived beneath the shrivel'd rind;
Then climbs the branches with increasing strength,
Spreads as they spread, and lengthens with their
    length;
—Thus the slight wound ingraved on glass unneal'd
Runs in white lines along the lucid field;
Crack follows crack, to laws elastic just,
And the frail fabric shivers into dust.'

               ERASMUS DARWIN (1731–1802)
       From *The Economy of Vegetation* (Canto IV)

28 How to Grow Cucumbers

The stable yields a stercoraceous heap,
Impregnated with quick fermenting salts,
And potent to resist the freezing blast:
For ere the beech and elm have cast their leaf
Deciduous, when now November dark
Checks vegetation in the torpid plant
Exposed to his cold breath, the task begins.
Warily therefore, and with prudent heed,
He seeks a favour'd spot; that where he builds
The agglomerated pile, his frame may front
The sun's meridian disk, and at the back
Enjoy close shelter, wall, or reeds, or hedge
Impervious to the wind. First he bids spread
Dry fern or litter'd hay, that may imbibe
The ascending damps; then leisurely impose,
And lightly shaking it with agile hand
From the full fork, the saturated straw.
What longest binds the closest, forms secure
The shapely side, that as it rises takes,
By just degrees, an over-hanging breadth,

[53]

Sheltering the base with its projected eaves.
The uplifted frame compact at every joint,
And overlaid with clear translucent glass,
He settles next upon the sloping mount,
Whose sharp declivity shoots off secure
From the dash'd pane the deluge as it falls:
He shuts it close, and the first labour ends.

★ ★ ★

The seed, selected wisely, plump, and smooth,
And glossy, he commits to pots of size
Diminutive, well filled with well-prepared
And fruitful soil, that has been treasured long
And drank no moisture from the dripping clouds:
These on the warm and genial earth that hides
The smoking manure, and o'erspreads it all,
He places lightly, and as time subdues
The rage of fermentation, plunges deep
In the soft medium, till they stand immersed.
Then rise the tender germs, upstarting quick
And spreading wide their spongy lobes, at first
Pale, wan, and livid, but assuming soon,
If fann'd by balmy and nutritious air,
Strain'd through the friendly mats, a vivid green.
Two leaves produced, two rough indented leaves,
Cautious he pinches from the second stalk
A pimple, that portends a future sprout,
And interdicts its growth. Thence straight succeed
The branches, sturdy to his utmost wish,
Prolific all, and harbingers of more.
The crowded roots demand enlargement now,
And transplantation in an ampler space.
Indulged in what they wish, they soon supply
Large foliage, overshadowing golden flowers,
Blown on the summit of the apparent fruit.
These have their sexes, and when summer shines
The bee transports the fertilising meal
From flower to flower, and even the breathing air
Wafts the rich prize to its appointed use.

[54]

Not so when winter scowls. Assistant art
Then acts in Nature's office, brings to pass
The glad espousals, and ensures the crop.

WILLIAM COWPER (1731–1800)
From *The Task* (Book III: 'The Garden')

4 Useful for Lovers (Male)

29 A Charme, or an Allay for Love

If so be a Toad be laid
In a Sheeps-skin newly flaid,
And that ty'd to a man 'twil sever
Him and his affections ever.

ROBERT HERRICK (1591–1674)

30 The Advice

Wou'd you in Love succeed, be Brisk, be Gay,
Cast all dull Thoughts and serious Looks away;
Think not with down cast Eyes, and mournful Air,
To move to pity, the Relentless Fair,
Or draw from her bright Eyes a Christal Tear.
This Method Foreign is to your Affair,
Too formal for the Frolick you prepare:
Thus, when you think she yields to Love's advance,
You'll find 'tis no Consent, but Complaisance.
Whilst he who boldly rifles all her Charms,
Kisses and Ravishes her in his Arms,
Seizes the favour, stays not for a Grant,
Alarms her Blood, and makes her sigh and pant;
Gives her no time to speak, or think't a Crime,
Enjoys his Wish, and well imploys his time.

CHARLES SACKVILLE, EARL OF DORSET (1638–1706)

31 Advice to the Old Beaux

Scrape no more your harmless Chins,
  Old Beaux, in hope to please;
You shou'd repent your former Sins,
  Not study their Increase;
Young awkward Fops, may shock our Sight,
But you offend by Day and Night.

In vain the Coachman turns about
  And whips the dappl'd Greys;
When the old Ogler looks out,
  We turn away our Face.
True Love and Youth will ever charm,
But both affected, cannot warm.

Summer-fruits we highly prise,
  They kindly cool the Blood;
But Winter-berries we despise,
  And leave 'em in the Wood;
On the Bush they may look well,
But gather'd, lose both taste and smell.

That you languish, that you dye,
  Alas, is but too true;
Yet tax not us with Cruelty.
  Who daily pity you.
Nature henceforth alone accuse,
In vain we grant, if she refuse.
                    SIR CHARLES SEDLEY (1639–1701)

32 *From* the First Book of Ovid's Art of Love

You, who in Cupid's rolls inscribe your name,
First seek an object worthy of your flame;
Then strive, with art, your lady's mind to gain;
And, last, provide your love may long remain.
On these three precepts all my works shall move;
These are the rules and principles of love.
　Before your youth with marriage is opprest,
Make choice of one who suits your humour best;
And such a damsel drops not from the sky,
She must be sought for with a curious eye.
　The wary angler, in the winding brook,
Knows what the fish, and where to bait his hook.
The fowler and the huntsman know by name
The certain haunts and harbour of their game.
So must the lover beat the likeliest grounds;
The assembly where his quarry most abounds.
Nor shall my novice wander far astray;
These rules shall put him in the ready way.
Thou shalt not sail around the continent,
As far as Perseus, or as Paris went;
For Rome alone affords thee such a store,
As all the world can hardly show thee more:
The face of heaven with fewer stars is crowned,
Than beauties in the Roman sphere are found.
　Whether thy love is bent on blooming youth,
On dawning sweetness in unartful truth,
Or courts the juicy joys of riper growth;
Here may'st thou find thy full desires in both.
Or if autumnal beauties please thy sight,
(An age that knows to give, and take delight,)
Millions of matrons of the graver sort,
In common prudence, will not balk the sport.

★　★　★

To enjoy the maid, will that thy suit advance?

'Tis a hard question, and a doubtful chance.
One maid, corrupted, bawds the better for't;
Another for herself would keep the sport.
Thy business may be furthered or delayed;
But, by my counsel, let alone the maid;
Even though she should consent to do the feat,
The profit's little, and the danger great.
I will not lead thee through a rugged road,
But, where the way lies open, safe, and broad.
Yet if thou find'st her very much thy friend,
And her good face her diligence commend,
Let the fair mistress have thy first embrace,
And let the maid come after in her place.

★　★　★

But dress not like a fop, nor curl your hair,
Nor with a pumice make your body bare;
Leave those effeminate and useless toys
To eunuchs, who can give no solid joys.
Neglect becomes a man; thus Theseus found;
Uncurled, uncombed, the nymph his wishes crowned.
The rough Hippolytus was Phaedra's care;
And Venus thought the rude Adonis fair.
Be not too finical; but yet be clean,
And wear well-fashioned clothes, like other men.
Let not your teeth be yellow, or be foul,
Nor in wide shoes your feet too loosely roll;
Of a black muzzle, and long beard, beware,
And let a skilful barber cut your hair;
Your nails be picked from filth, and even pared,
Nor let your nasty nostrils bud with beard;
Cure your unsavoury breath, gargle your throat,
And free your armpits from the ram and goat:
Dress not, in short, too little or too much;
And be not wholly French, nor wholly Dutch.

Translated by JOHN DRYDEN (1631–1700)

33 Proverbial Advice to Gentlemen

He that would the daughter win,
Must with the mother first begin.

A woman, a dog and a walnut tree—
The more you beat them, the better they'll be.

34 *From* The Art of Dancing

Now haste, my Muse, pursue thy destin'd way,
What dresses best become the dancer, say;
The rules of dress forget not to impart,
A lesson previous to the dancing art.
  The soldier's scarlet, glowing from afar,
Shows that his bloody occupation's war;
Whilst the lawn band, beneath a double chin,
As plainly speaks divinity within;
The milk-maid safe through driving rains and snows,
Wrapp'd in her cloak, and prop'd on pattens goes;
While the soft belle, immur'd in velvet chair,
Needs but the silken shoe, and trusts her bosom bare:
The woolly drab, and English broad-cloth warm,
Guard well the horseman from the beating storm,
But load the dancer with too great a weight,
And call from ev'ry pore the dewy sweat;
Rather let him his active limbs display
In camblet thin, or glossy paduasoy,
Let no unwieldy pride his shoulders press,
But airy, light, and easy be his dress;
Thin be his yielding sole, and low his heel,
So shall he nimbly bound, and safely wheel.

But let not precepts known my verse prolong,
Precepts which use will better teach than song;
For why should I the gallant spark command,
With clean white gloves to fit his ready hand?
Or in his fob enlivening spirits wear,
And pungent salts to raise the fainting fair?
Or hint, the sword that dangles at his side
Should from its silken bondage be unty'd?
Why should my lays the youthful tribe advise,
Lest snowy clouds from out their wigs arise:
So shall their partners mourn their laces spoil'd,
And shiny silks with greasy powder soil'd?
Nor need I, sure, bid prudent youths beware,
Lest with erected tongues their buckles stare,
The pointed steel shall oft their stockings rend,
And oft th'approaching petticoat offend.

SOAME JENYNS (1704–87)

35 *From* The Yeomen of the Guard

A man who would woo a fair maid,
Should 'prentice himself to the trade;
   And study all day,
   In methodical way,
How to flatter, cajole, and persuade.
He should 'prentice himself at fourteen,
And practise from morning to e'en;
   And when he's of age,
   If he will, I'll engage,
He may capture the heart of a queen!
     It is purely a matter of skill,
      Which all may attain if they will:
       But every Jack
       He must study the knack
      If he wants to make sure of his Jill!

USEFUL FOR LOVERS (MALE)

If he's made the best use of his time,
His twig he'll so carefully lime
    That every bird
    Will come down at his word,
Whatever its plumage and clime.
He must learn that the thrill of a touch
May mean little, or nothing, or much;
    It's an instrument rare,
    To be handled with care,
And ought to be treated as such.
    It is purely a matter of skill,
    Which all may attain if they will:
      But every Jack,
      He must study the knack
    If he wants to make sure of his Jill!

Then a glance may be timid or free;
It will vary in mighty degree,
    From an impudent stare
    To a look of despair
That no maid without pity can see.
And a glance of despair is no guide—
It may have its ridiculous side;
    It may draw you a tear
    Or a box on the ear;
You can never be sure till you've tried.
    It is purely a matter of skill,
    Which all may attain if they will:
      But every Jack
      He must study the knack
    If he wants to make sure of his Jill!

W. S. GILBERT (1836–1911)

5 Useful for Lovers (Female)

36 To Women, to Hide Their Teeth, if They be Rotten or Rusty

Close keep your lips, if that you meane
To be accounted inside cleane:
For if you cleave them, we shall see
There in your teeth much Leprosie.

ROBERT HERRICK (1591–1674)

37 Advice to the Ladies

Who now regards Chloris, her tears, and her whining,
Her sighs, and fond wishes, and aukward repining?
What a pother is here, with her amorous glances,
Soft fragments of Ovid, and scrapes of romances!

An nice prude at fifteen! and a romp in decay!
Cold December affects the sweet blossoms of May;
To fawn in her dotage, and in her bloom spurn us,
Is to quench Love's bright torch, and with touchwood to
  burn us.

Believe me, dear maids, there's no way of evading;
While ye pish, and cry nay, your roses are fading:
Though your passion survive, your beauty will dwindle,
And our languishing embers can never rekindle.

When bright in your zeniths, we prostrate before ye,
When ye set in a cloud, what fool will adore ye?
Then, ye fair, be advis'd, and snatch the kind blessing,
And show your good conduct by timely possessing.

WILLIAM SOMERVILE (1675–1742)

38 Traditional Charms for Finding the Identity of One's True Love

New moon, new moon, I hail thee!
By all the virtue in thy body,
Grant this night that I may see
He who my true love is to be.

Hoping this night my true love to see,
I place my shoes in the form of a T.

> *(On 28 October a young girl should recite the following rhyme, turn round three times and throw an apple-paring over her left shoulder. The paring should land forming an initial.)*

St Simon and Jude, on you I intrude,
  By this paring I hold to discover,
Without any delay, to tell me this day
  The first letter of my own true lover.

Last May-day fair I search'd to find a snail,
That might my secret lover's name reveal;
Upon a gooseberry bush a snail I found,
For always snails near sweetest fruit abound.

[64]

I seiz'd the vermin, home I quickly sped,
And on the hearth the milk-white embers spread.
Slow crawl'd the snail, and if I right can spell,
In the soft ashes mark'd a curious L;
Oh, may this wondrous omen lucky prove,
For L is found in Lubberkin and Love!

JOHN GAY (1685–1732)
From *Shepherd's Week*

39 *From* The Shepherd's Calendar

Or, trying simple charms and spells,
Which rural superstition tells,
They pull the little blossom threads
From out the knotweed's button heads,
And put the husk, with many a smile,
In their white bosoms for a while.
Then if they guess aright the swain
Their love's sweet fancies try to gain,
'Tis said that ere it lies an hour,
'Twill blossom with a second flower,
And from the bosom's handkerchief
Bloom as it ne'er had lost a leaf.

JOHN CLARE (1793–1864)

40 Written in an Ovid

Ovid is the surest guide
　You can name, to show the way
To any woman, maid or bride,
　Who resolves to go astray.

MATTHEW PRIOR (1664–1721)

[65]

41 *From* Ovid's Third Book of The Art of Love

Wherein he recommends the rules and instructions to the Fair-Sex in the Conduct of their Amours.

Attend, ye nymphs, by wedlock unconfin'd,
And hear my precepts, while she prompts my mind:
Ev'n now, in bloom of youth, and beauty's prime,
Beware of coming age, nor waste your time:
Now, while you may, and ripening years invite,
Enjoy the seasonable, sweet delight:
For rolling years, like stealing waters, glide:
Nor hope to stop their ever-ebbing tide:
Think not hereafter will the loss repay;
For every morrow will the taste decay,
And leave less relish than the former day.

* * *

The hair dispos'd, may gain or lose a grace,
And much become, or misbecome, the face.
What suits your features, of your glass inquire;
For no one rule is fix'd for head-attire.
A face too long should part and flat the hair,
Lest, upward comb'd, the length too much appear:
So Laodamia dress'd. A face too round
Should show the ears, and with a tower be crown'd.
On either shoulder, one her locks displays;
Adorn'd like Phoebus, when he sings his lays:
Another, all her tresses ties behind;
So dress'd, Diana hunts the fearful hind.
Dishevell'd locks most graceful are to some;
Others, the binding fillets more become:
Some plait, like spiral shells, their braided hair,
Others, the loose and waving curl prefer.
But to recount the several dresses worn,
Which artfully each several face adorn,
Were endless, as to tell the leaves on trees,
The beasts on Alpine hills, or Hybla's bees.

Many there are, who seem to slight all care,
And with pleasing negligence ensnare;
Whose mornings oft in such a dress are spent,
And all is art that looks like accident.

* * *

I need not warn you of too powerful smells,
Which sometimes health, or kindly heat, expels.
Nor from your tender legs to pluck with care
The casual growth of all unseemly hair.
Though not to nymphs of Caucasus I sing,
Nor such who taste remote the Mysian spring;
Yet, let me warn you, that, through no neglect,
You let your teeth disclose the least defect.
You know the use of white to make you fair,
And how, with red, lost colour to repair,
Imperfect eyebrows you by art can mend,
And skin, when wanting, o'er a scar extend.
Nor need the fair-one be asham'd, who tries,
By art, to add new lustre to her eyes.
A little book I've made, but with great care,
How to preserve the face, and how repair.
In that, the nymphs, by time or chance annoy'd,
May see, what pains to please them I've employ'd.
But, still beware, that from your lover's eye
You keep conceal'd the med'cines you apply:
Though art assists, yet must that art be hid,
Lest, whom it would invite, it should forbid.
Who would not take offence, to see a face
All daub'd, and dripping with the melted grease?
And tho' your unguents bear th'Athenian name,
The wool's unsavoury scent is still the same.
Marrow of stags, not your pomatums try,
Nor clean your furry teeth, when men are by;
For many things, when done, afford delight,
Which yet, while doing, may offend the sight.

* * *

Faults in your person, or your face, correct:

[67]

And few are seen that have not some defect.
The nymph too short, her seat should seldom quit,
Lest when she stands, she may be thought to sit;
And when extended on her couch she lies,
Let the length of petticoats conceal her size.
The lean of thick-wrought stuff her clothes should choose,
And fuller made, than what the plumper use.
If pale, let her the crimson juice apply,
If swarthy, to the Pharian varnish fly.
A leg too lank, tight garters still must wear;
Nor should an ill-shaped foot be ever bare.
Round shoulders, bolster'd, will appear the least;
And lacing strait, confines too full a breast.
Whose fingers are too fat, and nails too coarse,
Should always shun much gesture in discourse.
And you, whose breath is touch'd, this caution take,
Nor fasting, nor too near another, speak.
Let not the nymph with laughter much abound,
Whose teeth are black, uneven, or unsound.
You hardly think how much on this depends,
Or how a laugh, or spoils a face, or mends.
Gape not too wide, lest you disclose your gums,
And lose the dimple which the cheek becomes.
Nor let your sides too strong concussions shake,
Lest you the softness of the sex forsake.
In some, distortions quite the face disguise;
Another laughs, that you would think she cries.
In one, too hoarse a voice we hear betray'd,
Another's is as harsh as if she bray'd.

                    Translated by WILLIAM CONGREVE (1670–1729)

42 Advice to a Lady in Autumn

Asses' milk, half a pint, take at seven, or before,
Then sleep for an hour or two, and no more.
At nine stretch your arms, and, oh! think when alone
There's no pleasure in bed. — Mary, bring me my gown.
Slip on that ere you rise; let your caution be such;
Keep all cold from your breast, there's already too much;
Your pinners set right, your twitcher tied on,
Your prayers at an end, and your breakfast quite done,
Retire to some author improving and gay,
And with sense like your own, set your mind for the day.
At twelve you may walk, for at this time o' the year,
The sun, like your wit, is as mild as 'tis clear:
But mark in the meadows the ruin of time;
Take the hint, and let life be improved in its prime.
Return not in haste, nor of dressing take heed;
For beauty like yours no assistance can need.
With an appetite thus down to dinner you sit,
Where the chief of the feast is the flow of your wit:
Let this be indulged, and let laughter go round;
As it pleases your mind to your health 'twill redound.
After dinner two glasses at least, I approve;
Name the first to the King, and the last to your love:
Thus cheerful, with wisdom, with innocence, gay,
And calm with your joys, gently glide through the day.
The dews of the evening most carefully shun;
Those tears of the sky for the loss of the sun.
Then in chat, or at play, with a dance or a song,
Let the night, like the day, pass with pleasure along.
All cares, but of love, banish far from your mind;
And those you may end, when you please to be kind.

PHILIP STANHOPE, EARL OF CHESTERFIELD (1694–1773)

43 *From* The Art of Dancing

Dare I in such momentous points advise,
I should condemn the hoop's enormous size:
Of ills I speak by long experience found,
Oft have I trod th'immeasurable round,
And mourn'd my shins bruis'd black with many a wound.
Nor should the tighten'd stays, too straitly lac'd,
In whalebone bondage gall the slender waist;
Nor waving lappets should the dancing fair,
Nor ruffles edg'd with dangling fringes wear;
Oft will the cobweb ornaments catch hold
On th'approaching button rough with gold,
Nor force nor art can then the bonds divide,
When once th'entangled Gordian knot is ty'd.
So the unhappy pair, by Hymen's pow'r,
Together join'd in some ill-fated hour,
The more they strive their freedom to regain,
The faster binds th'indissoluble chain.
    Let each fair maid, who fears to be disgrac'd,
Ever be sure to tie her garters fast,
Lest the loos'd string, amidst the public ball,
A wish'd-for prize to some proud fop should fall,
Who the rich treasure shall triumphant show;
And with warm blushes cause her cheeks to glow.

SOAME JENYNS (1704–87)

44 Time's Revenges

*(A straight talk addressed by a middle-aged bachelor to the
love of his youth)*

No, Honoria, I am greatly flattered
  When you cast a soft, seductive eye
On a figure permanently battered
  Out of shape by Anno Domini;
    Yet, you'll take it please, from me,
    It can never, never be.

Vainly,—and you mustn't be offended
  Should a certain candour mark my words—
Vainly is the obvious net extended
  Underneath the eyes of us old birds;
    Nor are we—it sounds unkind—
    Taking any salt behind.

You have passed, you say, the salad season,
  Growing sick of boyhood's callow fluff;
You prefer the age of settled reason—
  Men with minds composed of sterner stuff;
    All your nature, now so ripe,
    Yearns towards the finished type.

Yes, but what about your full-fledged fogeys?
  Youth is good enough for us, I guess;
Still we like it fluffy; still the vogue is
  Sweet-and-Twenty—ay, or even less;
    Only lately I have been
    Badly hit by Seventeen.

I have known my heart to melt like tallow
  In the company of simple youth,
Careless though its brain was clearly shallow,
  Beauty being tantamount to Truth;
    Give us freshness, free of art,
    We'll supply the brainy part.

Thus in *your* hands I was soft as putty,
  Ere your intellect began to grow,
When we went a-Maying in the nutty
    Time—it seems a thousand years ago;
      Then I wished to make you mine;
      Why on earth did you decline?

You declined because you had a notion
  You could choose a husband when you would;
There were better fish inside the ocean
    Than had come to hand—or quite as good;
      So, until you reached the thirties,
      We were treated much as dirt is.

Then you grew a little less fastidious,
  Wondering if your whale would soon arrive,
Till your summers (age is so insidious)
    Touched their present total—45;
      Well, then, call it 38;
      Anyhow, it's *far* too late.

You may say there's something most unknightly
  Something almost rude about my tone?
No, Honoria, when regarded rightly,
    These are Time's revenges, not my own;
      You may deem it want of tact,
      Still, I only state the fact.

Yet, to end upon a note less bitter,
  You shall hear what chokes me off to-day:
'Tis the thought (it makes my heart-strings twitter)
    Of a Young Thing chasing nuts in May:
      'Tis my loyalty to Her,
      To the Girl that once you were.

                    OWEN SEAMAN (1861–1936)
                    From *Punch*

45 Social Note

Lady, lady, should you meet
One whose ways are all discreet,
One who murmurs that his wife
Is the lodestar of his life,
One who keeps assuring you
That he never was untrue,
Never loved another one . . .
   Lady, lady, better run!
   DOROTHY PARKER (1893–1967)

46 Unfortunate Coincidence

By the time you swear you're his,
  Shivering and sighing,
And he vows his passion is
  Infinite, undying—
Lady, make a note of this:
  One of you is lying.
   DOROTHY PARKER (1893–1967)

47 News Item

Men seldom make passes
At girls who wear glasses.
  DOROTHY PARKER
   (1893–1967)

6 Useful for Those Contemplating Matrimony

48 Proverbial Advice on Marriage

Marry in Lent,
Live to repent.

Marry in May,
Repent alway.

Who weds a sot to get his cot,
Will lose the cot and keep the sot.

Like blood, like good, and like age
Make the happiest marriage.

49 *From* Hesiod's Works and Days (*Book II*)

Next to my counsels an attention pay,
To form your judgement for the nuptial day.
When you have number'd thrice ten years in time,
The age mature when manhood dates his prime,
With caution choose the partner of your bed:
Whom fifteen springs have crown'd, a virgin wed.
Let prudence now direct your choice; a wife
Is or a blessing, or a curse, in life;

Her father, mother, know, relations, friends,
For on her education much depends:
If all are good accept the maiden bride;
Then form her manners, and her actions guide:
A life of bliss succeeds the happy choice;
Nor shall your friends lament, nor foes rejoice.
Wretched the man condemn'd to drag the chain,
What restless ev'nings his, what days of pain!
Of a luxurious mate, a wanton dame,
That ever burns with an insatiate flame,
A wife who seeks to revel out the nights.
In sumptuous banquets, and in stol'n delights:
Ah! wretched mortal! tho in body strong,
Thy constitution cannot serve thee long;
Old age vexatious shall o'ertake thee soon;
Thine is the ev'n of life before the noon.

Translated by THOMAS COOKE, known as
'HESIOD' COOKE (1703–56)

50 *From* Townley Plays: *No. 12* Shepherd's Play

It is sayde full ryfe★
A man may not wyfe
And also thryfe,
And all in a yere.

ANON (c. 1388)

★often

[75]

51 On Marriage

How happy a thing were a wedding,
  And a bedding,
If a man might purchase a wife
  For a twelvemonth and a day;
But to live with her all a man's life,
  For ever and for aye,
Till she grows as grey as a cat,
Good faith, Mr. Parson, excuse me from that!

THOMAS FLATMAN (1635–88)

52 How to Choose a Wife

Good sir, if you will shew the best of your skill
  To picke a vertuous creature,
Then picke such a wife, as you love a life,
  Of a comely grace and feature;
The noblest part let it be her heart,
  Without deceit or cunning,
With a nimble wit, and all things fit,
  With a tongue that's never running,
The haire of her head, it must not be red,
  But faire and brown as a berry;
Her fore-head high, with a christall eye,
  Her lips as red as a cherry.

ANON

From Wit's Recreations, 1645

53 Against Marriage to His Mistress

Yes, all the world must sure agree,
He who's secured of having thee,
　　Will be entirely blessed;
But 'twere in me too great a wrong,
To make one who has been so long
　　My queen, my slave at last.

Nor ought those things to be confined,
That were for public good designed:
　　Could we, in foolish pride,
Make the sun always with us stay,
'Twould burn our corn and grass away,
　　To starve the world beside.

Let not the thoughts of parting fright
Two souls which passion does unite;
　　For while our love does last,
Neither will strive to go away;
And why the devil should we stay,
　　When once that love is past?
　　　　　　WILLIAM WALSH (1663–1708)

54 Close Season for Marriage

*(Forbidden dates in English Church until the
interregnum)*

Advent marriage doth thee deny,
But Hilary gives thee liberty.
Septuagesima says thee nay,
Eight days from Easter says you may.
Rogation bids thee to contain,
But Trinity sets thee free again.
　　　　　　　　　　ANON

[77]

55 Marriage

Those awful words, "Till death do part,'
May well alarm the youthful heart:
No after-thought when once a wife;
The die is cast, and cast for life;
Yet thousands venture ev'ry day,
As some base passion leads the way.
Pert Silvia talks of wedlock-scenes,
Tho' hardly enter'd on her teens;
Smiles on her whining spark, and hears
The sugar'd speech with raptur'd ears;
Impatient of a parent's rule,
She leaves her sire and weds a fool.
Want enters at the guardless door,
And Love is fled, to come no more.

NATHANIEL COTTON (1705–88)
From *Visions in Verse* (VII)

56 Propitious Days for Weddings

Monday for wealth,
Tuesday for health,
Wednesday the best day of all;
Thursday for crosses,
Friday for losses,
Saturday no luck at all.

ANON

57 Surnames to be Avoided in Marriage

To change the name, and not the letter,
Is a change for the worse, and not for the better.

ANON

58 On Ladies' Accomplishments

Your dressing, dancing, gadding, where's the good in?
Sweet lady, tell me—can you make a pudding?

ANON (1740)

59 Marriages

Disposed to wed, e'en while you hasten, stay;
There's great advantage in a small delay:—
Thus Ovid sang, and much the wise approve
This prudent maxim of the priest of Love:
If poor, delay for future want prepares,
And eases humble life of half its cares;
If rich, delay shall brace the thoughtful mind,
T' endure the ills that e'en the happiest find:
Delay shall knowledge yield on either part,
And show the value of the vanquish'd heart;
The humours, passions, merits, failings prove,
And gently raise the veil that's worn by Love;
Love, that impatient guide!—too proud to think
Of vulgar wants, of clothing, meat and drink,
Urges our amorous swains their joys to seize,
And then, at rags and hunger frighten'd, flees:—
Yet not too long in cold debate remain;
Till age refrain not—but if old refrain.

GEORGE CRABBE (1754–1832)
From *The Parish Register* (Part II)

[79]

60 The Perfect Husband

He tells you when you've got on
    too much lipstick,
And helps you with your girdle
    when your hips stick.

OGDEN NASH (1902–70)

61 Responsibility

'Tis easy enough to be twenty-one:
'Tis easy enough to marry;
But when you try both games at once
'Tis a bloody big load to carry.

ANON

7 Useful for Those Contemplating Children

62 A Scottish Proverb

He's a fool that marries at Yule,
For when the corn's to shear the bairn's to bear.

63 Observation

Who to the North, or South, doth set
His Bed, Male children shall beget.
ROBERT HERRICK (1591–1674)

64 The Best Time for Conception

Hold, furious Youth—Better thy Heat assuage,
And moderate a while thy eager Rage;
For if the Genial Sport you now complete,
Full of the Fumes of undigested Meat,
A thin diluted Substance shalt thou place,
Too weak a Basis for a Manly Grace
To rise in Figure just, and dignify thy Race.
Advis'd, defer the Work, till Time produce
A more mature, and well-concocted Juice.
Hard is the Rule, and Lovers oft complain;
Tho hard, yet proper for a vig'rous Strain.
CLAUDE QUILLET (1602–61)

65 How to Conceive Boys

Again, the Morning for a *Male* is best;
The Seed maturing in the Time of Rest,
A firm and well-cemented Basis lays,
From whence the lusty nervous Boy to raise.

Nor must thou only this thy Care believe,
That the close Womb the fruitful Seed receive:
But when the Streams of either Parent mix'd,
Are in their proper Receptacle fix'd;
Let the *Wife*, mindful of the kind Design,
Turn to the *Right*, and there at Ease recline:
For in that Cell, the Seeds of Life begun,
Will surest work the *Fluid* to a *Son*.
Who knows not that the *Right* the *Left* excels,
That there superior Heat and Vigour dwells;
From thence new Life distends each sinking Vein,
And re-inspires the languid Pulse again?
Hence they who *Nature* with Attention read,
Think from the *Right* the vig'rous Males proceed.

Some too who would advance *the Rules of Love*,
Defective Nature thus by Art improve;
They the *left Testicle* with force restrain,
That Nature may a fuller Stream maintain,
And thro the *Right* the whole collected Tide,
Rushing with more prolifick Virtue, glide.
So when the *Swains* a lusty Race intend,
That scorn beneath the mighty *Yoke* to bend;
Soon as the youngest of the *Herd* they find,
They fast the *Left*, and weakest Vessels bind;
And thus secur'd, he multiplies his Kind.
Such Care to propagate the Male obtains,
And through each Species undistinguish'd reigns.

CLAUDE QUILLET (1602–61)

64 and 65 from *Callipaedia, or the Art of Getting Beautiful
Children* (Book II). Published in Latin in Paris, 1656

Translated by GEORGE SEWELL (1688?–1726)

66 Cravings during Pregnancy

But Teeming Women, when Desire grows strong,
Are apt for ev'ry thing they see to Long.
Sand, Chalk, and Dirt, their Appetite provoke,
The Hearth's black Ashes, and the Chimney's Smoke.
Nay, once I saw a Pregnant Wife devour
A living Chick, and lick its reeking Gore:
Cackling she seiz'd it, in the flut'ring Brood,
And tore its Flesh alive, and suck'd its Blood;
Bone, Feathers, Garbidge in her Mouth were seen
And Putid Clotts defil'd her Breasts obscene.

M. SAINT-MARTHE (fl. 1580)

67 Labour

Your Hour approaching, to *Latona* cry,
And let a Midwife for your Help be nigh.
Your Labour let her aid, and both take Care
To bring the Child uninjur'd forth, and Fair.
Let her with Hand and Word assist your Throws;
She best your Ills, and how to help 'em, knows.
The Belly 'noint with Oils, and secret Seat
Of Lovers Joys unloose with kindly Heat.
Make clear the Passage for the Child to come
Thro' the streight Channel of the Opening Womb.
Whether your Limbs you on a Bed repose,
Or in a Chair expect the Parent Throws,
Ne'er to the Fury of the Pain give way;
For Fear and Weakness will the Birth delay.
If of your self you have so much Command,
Since standing is the proper Posture, stand.
The Child is in a narrow'r Passage torn,
But fair and perfect in a wider Born.

[83]

You must not, when your Labour's strong, be nice,
But with your utmost Spread expand your Thighs,
Extend your Arms, and urge the Infant's Way,
The sooner he'll behold the Promis'd Day.

M. SAINT-MARTHE (fl. 1580)
66 and 67 from *Paedotrophiae, or the Art of Bringing
Up Children* (Book I)
Translated anonymously, 1718

68 A Scottish Proverb

Waly, waly! bairns are bonny;
One's enough, and twa's too mony.

8 Useful for the Upbringing of Children

69 Note on Feeding

Breast
Is best.

ANON

70 Choosing a Wet-Nurse

If Health and Strength permit thee, don't refuse
The Child thy Nipple; nor another's use:
If to the Babe thou dost thy own deny,
Ill, will a venal Pap its Wants supply;
Ill, will the Bus'ness by that Nurse be done,
Who for another's Child neglects her own.
Yet, if thou'rt sickly, if thy Spirits fail,
If the Child's touch'd with any catching Ail,
This Duty, whether hated or desir'd,
Cease, and 'tis no more of thee requir'd.
Then not to Suckle, is not to neglect,
But chuse a Nurse, and I'll thy Choice direct.
A middle Age is best, nor Old nor Young,
Fresh be her Colour, and her Body strong;
Active and Healthy let her be, and Clean;
In Flesh, not over Fat, nor over Lean;
Long be her Neck, and broad her snowy Chest;
Her Arms of full Extent, and Plump her Breast.
Let on each Pap a ruddy Nipple bud,
And the Twin-Hillocks strut with vary'd Blood.
The Babe's delighted with a flowing Feast:
The sweetest and the whitest Milk is best.

[85]

If 'tis of an ungrateful Smell, be sure
Those Fountains to avoid, for they're impure.
Or if it sticks, when by the Finger try'd,
'Tis bad; nor should it thence too swiftly glide.

M. SAINT-MARTHE (fl. 1580)
From *Paedotrophiae, or the Art of Bringing Up
Children* (Book II)
Translated anonymously, 1718

71 Love between Brothers and Sisters

Whatever brawls disturb the street,
    There should be peace at home;
Where sisters dwell and brothers meet,
    Quarrels should never come.

Birds in their little nests agree,
    And 'tis a shameful sight,
When children of one family,
    Fall out and chide and fight.

Hard names at first and threat'ning words,
    That are but noisy breath,
May grow to clubs and naked swords,
    To murder and to death.

ISAAC WATTS (1674–1748)

72 To a Little Boy, who Had Destroyed a Nest of Young Birds

O cruel!—could thy infant bosom find
No pleasure but in other's misery?
Come, let me tear *thee* from thy parents' arms,

As thou hast torn these half-fledged innocents,
And dash thee naked on the cold bare stones,
All in thy tender mother's aching sight. —
But thou art young, and knowest not yet the cares,
The pangs, the feelings of an anxious parent,
Else would thy heart, by sad experience taught,
Weep o'er the little ruined family,
And mourn the ill thy cruel hand has done.

ANON
From *The Political Primer*, 1817

73 Temperance Song

(To be repeated by a boy)

Ladies and Gentlemen,
  List to my song;
Hurrah for temperance
  All the day long;
I'll taste not, handle not,
Touch not the wine,
  For every little boy like me
The temperance pledge should sign.

I'm a temperance boy,
  Just six years old,
And I love temperance
  Better than gold;
I'll taste not, handle not . . . etc.

Let every little boy
  Remember my song,
For God loves the children
  That never do wrong.
I'll taste not, handle not . . . etc.

ANON
From *The Temperance Orator and Reciter*,
19th century

[87]

74 I'll Never Use Tobacco

(To be repeated by a boy)

'I'll never use tobacco, no,
    It is a filthy weed!
I'll never put it in my mouth,'
    Said little Robert Reid.

'Why, there was idle Jerry Jones,
    As dirty as a pig,
Who smoked when only ten years old,
    And thought it made him big.

'He'd puff along the open street,
    As if he had no shame;
He'd sit beside the tavern-door,
    And there'd he'd do the same.

'He spent his time and money too,
    And made his mother sad;
She feared a worthless man would come
    From such a worthless lad.

'Oh no, I'll never smoke or chew,
    'Tis very wrong, indeed;
It hurts the health, it makes bad breath,'
    Said Little Robert Reid.

ANON

From *The Temperance Orator and Reciter*,
                            19th century

75 The Results of Stealing a Pin

A lad when at school, one day stole a pin,
And said that no harm was in such a small sin,
He next stole a knife, and said 'twas a trifle;
Next thing he did was pockets to rifle,
Next thing he did was a house to break in,
The next thing—upon a gallows to swing.
So let us avoid all little sinnings,
Since such is the end of petty beginnings.

ANON
From *The Ranks of Life, for the Amusement
and Instruction of Youth*, 1821

76 Rules and Regulations

A short direction
To avoid dejection:
By variations
In occupations,
And prolongation
Of relaxation,
And combinations
Of recreations,
And disputation
On the state of the nation
In adaptation
To your station,
By invitations
To friends and relations,
By evitation
Of amputation,
By permutation
In conversation,
And deep reflection
You'll avoid dejection.

Learn well your grammar,
And never stammer,
Write well and neatly,
And sing most sweetly,
Be enterprising,
Love early rising,
Go walks of six miles,
Have ready quick smiles.
With lightsome laughter,
Soft flowing after.
Drink tea, not coffee;
Never eat toffy.
Eat bread with butter.
Once more, don't stutter.
Don't waste your money,
Abstain from honey.
Shut doors behind you,
(Don't slam them, mind you.)
Drink beer, not porter.
Don't enter the water,
Till to swim you are able.
Sit close to the table.
Take care of a candle.
Shut a door by the handle,
Don't push with your shoulder
Until you are older.
Lose not a button.
Refuse cold mutton,
Starve your canaries,
Believe in fairies.
If you are able,
Don't have a stable
With any mangers.
Be rude to strangers.

MORAL: 'Behave.'
LEWIS CARROLL (1832–98)
(Written c. 1845)

77 To George Pulling Buds

Don't pull that bud, it yet may grow
   As fine a flower as this;
Had this been pulled a month ago,
   We should its beauties miss.
You are yourself a bud, my blooming boy,
Weigh well the consequence, ere you destroy,
Lest for a present paltry sport, you kill a future joy.
ADELAIDE O'KEEFFE (1776–1855)

78 The Disappointment

In tears to her mother poor Harriet came,
   Let us listen to hear what she says:
'O see, dear mamma, it is pouring with rain,
   We cannot go out in the chaise.

'All the week I have longed for this holiday so,
   And fancied the minutes were hours;
And now that I'm dressed and all ready to go,
   Do look at those terrible showers!'

'I'm sorry, my dear,' her kind mother replied,
   'The rain disappoints us to-day;
But sorrow still more that you fret for a ride,
   In such an extravagant way.

'These slight disappointments are sent to prepare
   For what may hereafter befall;
For seasons of *real* disappointment and care,
   Which commonly happen to all.

'For just like to-day with its holiday lost,
    Is life and its comfort at best:
Our pleasures are blighted, our purposes crossed,
    To teach us it is not our rest.

'And when those distresses and crosses appear,
    With which you may shortly be tried
You'll wonder that ever you wasted a tear
    On merely the loss of a ride.

'But though the world's pleasures are fleeting and vain,
    Religion is lasting and true;
Real pleasure and peace in her paths you may gain,
    Nor will disappointment ensue.'

JANE TAYLOR (1783–1824)

79 Washing and Dressing

Ah! why will my dear little girl be so cross,
    And cry, and look sulky, and pout?
To lose her sweet smile is a terrible loss,
    I can't even kiss her without.

You say you don't like to be washed and be drest,
    But would you not wish to be clean?
Come, drive that long sob from your dear little breast,
    This face is not fit to be seen.

If the water is cold, and the brush hurts your head,
    And the soap has got into your eye,
Will the water grow warmer for all that you've said?
    And what good will it do you to cry?

It is not to tease you and hurt you, my sweet,
　　But only for kindness and care,
That I wash you, and dress you, and make you look neat,
　　And comb out your tanglesome hair.

I don't mind the trouble, if you would not cry,
　　But pay me for all with a kiss;
That's right—take the towel and wipe your wet eye,
　　I thought you'd be good after this.

ANNE TAYLOR (1782–1866)

80　Rather Too Good, Little Peggy!

A true story

　　'Oh, pray come in,
　　Mamma's within,
　　　　Pray do not stay out there,
　　It pours with rain,
　　I say again
　　　　Come in, and take a chair.'
Thus lisped little PEGGY, whilst holding the door,
To a poor ragged woman she'd ne'er seen before!

　　'Mamma's upstairs,
　　She always cares
　　　　For children that are poor,
　　Come in, I pray,
　　Out there don't stay,
　　　　For I must shut the door.'
In walked three poor children, all squalid and mean,
Whom PEGGY, so courteous, till now had not seen.

'Mamma, come down!
I'm not alone,
    I've asked them to come in,
I heard the knock,
Undid the lock:
    Here's bread, so pray begin.'

Mamma came down, and stood amazed!
    Whether to laugh, or angry be,
        She knew not well,
        And could not tell,
Till on the group she gazed,
    And thus the truth could see.

'Indeed, my lady, do believe,'
    The woman humbly said.
Mamma replied, 'Take all the bread;
    To see such misery I grieve, —
But must not let my child do thus,
    She is not four years old.
I'll give you money, clothes, a few,
    To shelter these from cold.'

The woman thanked the lady kind,
    And gratefully went out,
But Peggy could not comprehend,
    What this was all about!
'Why, dear mamma, was I not right,
    To ask them in to stay all night?'
'My child, your heart is understood;
    (How can I well explain!)
When indiscreet — we're call'd TOO GOOD.
    Never do so again.'
            ADELAIDE O'KEEFFE (1776–1855)
    From *Poems for Young Children*, 1849

81 The Story of Augustus who Would Not Have Any Soup

Augustus was a chubby lad;
Fat, ruddy cheeks Augustus had;
And everybody saw with joy
The plump and hearty, healthy boy.
He ate and drank as he was told,
And never let his soup get cold.
But one day, one cold winter's day,
He scream'd out—'Take the soup away!
O take the nasty soup away!
I won't have any soup to-day.'

Next day begins his tale of woes,
Quite lank and lean Augustus grows.
Yet though he feels so weak and ill,
The naughty fellow cries out still—
'Not any soup for me, I say:
O take the nasty soup away!
I won't have any soup to-day.'

The third day comes; O what a sin!
To make himself so pale and thin.
Yet, when the soup is put on table,
He screams, as loud as he is able,—
'Not any soup for me, I say:
O take the nasty soup away!
I won't have any soup to-day.'

Look at him, now the fourth day's come!
He scarcely weighs a sugar-plum;
He's like a little bit of thread,
And on the fifth day, he was—dead!
                    HEINRICH HOFFMAN (1809–74)
                         Translated anonymously

82 Self-Examination

Did I this morn devoutly pray
For God's assistance through the day?
And did I read His sacred Word,
To make my life therewith accord?
Did I for any purpose try
To hide the truth, or tell a lie?
Was I obedient, humble, mild—
To prove myself a Christian child?
Did I my thoughts with prudence guide,
Checking ill-humour, anger pride?
Did I my lips from aught refrain
That might my fellow-creatures pain?
Did I with cheerful patience bear
The little ills that all must share?
To all my duties through the day
Did I a due attention pay?
And did I, when the day was o'er,
God's watchful care again implore?
Saviour, Thy grace divine impart,
To feed my soul, and cleanse my heart,
And make me meet for heaven above,
To join Thy saints in praise and love.

ANON (19th century)

83 Table Rules for Little Folk

In silence I must take my seat
And give God thanks for what I eat,
Must for my food in patience wait
Till I am asked to hand my plate.
I must not scold, nor whine, nor pout,
Nor move my chair, nor plate about,

With knife, or fork, or napkin ring,
I must not play, nor must I sing.
I must not speak a useless word,
For children must be seen, not heard.
I must not talk about my food,
Nor fret, if I don't think it good.
I must not say 'the bread is old',
'The tea is hot'—'the coffee cold'.
I must not cry for this, or that,
Nor murmur if my meat be fat.
My mouth with food I mustn't crowd,
Nor while I'm eating speak aloud.
Must turn my head to cough, or sneeze,
And when I ask, say 'If you please'.
The table cloth I must not spoil,
Nor with my food my fingers soil.
Must keep my seat when I have done,
Nor round the table sport, or run.
When told to rise, then I must put
The chair away with noiseless foot.
And lift my heart to God above
In praise for all His wondrous love.

ANON

84 Kindness to Animals

Little children, never give
Pain to things that feel and live:
Let the gentle robin come
For the crumbs you save at home,—
As his meat you throw along
He'll repay you with a song;
Never hurt the timid hare
Peeping from her green grass lair,
Let her come and sport and play
On the lawn at close of day;

The little lark goes soaring high
To the bright windows of the sky,
Singing as if 'twere always spring,
And fluttering on an untired wing,—
Oh! let him sing his happy song,
Nor do these gentle creatures wrong.

ANON

85 Whole Duty of Children

A child should always say what's true
And speak when he is spoken to,
And behave mannerly at table;
At least as far as he is able.

ROBERT LOUIS STEVENSON
(1850–94)

86 Address to Children

My little dears, who learn to read, pray early learn to shun
That very silly thing indeed which people call a pun.
Read Entick's rules, and 'twill be found how simple an
    offence
It is to make the self-same sound afford a double sense.
For instance ale may make you ail, your aunt an ant may
    kill,
You in a vale may buy a veil, and Bill may pay the bill,
Or if to France your bark you steer, at Dover it may be
A peer appears upon the pier, who, blind, still goes to sea.
Thus one might say when to a treat good friends accept our
    greeting,
'Tis meet that men who meet to eat, should eat their meat
    when meeting.

Brawn on the board's no bore indeed, although from boar
    prepared,
Nor can the fowl on which we feed foul feeding be
    declared—
Most wealthy men good manors have, however vulgar
    they;
And actors still the harder slave, the oftener they play;
So poets can't the baize obtain unless their tailors choose,
While grooms and coachmen not in vain each evening seek
    the mews.
The dyer, who by dyeing lives, a dire life maintains;
The glazier, it is known, receives his profits from his panes;
By gardeners thyme is tied, 'tis true, when Spring is in its
    prime,
But time or tide won't wait for you, if you are tied for
    time.

ANON
From *The World of Wit and Humour*, 1883

87 What is Veal?

William asked how veal was made,
    His little sister smiled,
It grew in foreign climes, she said,
    And call'd him silly child.

Eliza, laughing at them both,
    Told, to their great surprise,
The meat cook boiled to make the broth,
    Once lived, had nose and eyes;

Nay, more, had legs, and walked about;
    William in wonder stood,
He could not make the riddle out,
    But begged his sister would.

[99]

Well, brother, I have had my laugh,
  And you shall have yours now,
Veal, when alive, was call'd a calf—
  Its mother was a cow.

ANON

From *Juvenile Poems*, 1841

88 The Cow

Come, children, listen to me now,
And you shall hear about the cow;
You'll find her useful, alive or dead,
Whether she's black, or white, or red.
When milk-maids milk her, morn or night,
She gives us *milk* so fresh and white;
And this, we little children think,
Is very nice for us to drink.

The curdled milk they press and squeeze,
And so they make it into *cheese*;
The cream they skim, and shake in churns,
And then it soon to *butter* turns.
And when she's dead, her flesh is good,
For *beef* is our true English food;
But though in health it makes us strong,
To eat too much is very wrong.

Then lime and bark the tanner takes,
And of her skin he *leather* makes;
And this we know they mostly use
To make us good strong boots and shoes;
And last of all, if cut with care,
Her horns make combs to comb our hair.
And so we learn, thanks to our teachers,
That cows are very useful creatures.

ANON (19th century)

[100]

89 Henry King

*Who chewed bits of String, and was early cut off in
Dreadful Agonies.*

The Chief Defect of Henry King
Was chewing little bits of String.
At last he swallowed some which tied
Itself in ugly Knots inside.
Physicians of the Utmost Fame
Were called at once; but when they came
They answered, as they took their Fees,
'There is no Cure for this Disease.
Henry will very soon be dead.'
His Parents stood about his Bed
Lamenting his Untimely Death,
When Henry, with his Latest Breath,
Cried—'Oh, my Friends, be warned by me,
That Breakfast, Dinner, Lunch, and Tea
Are all the Human Frame requires . . .'
With that, the Wretched Child expires.

HILAIRE BELLOC (1870–1953)

90 Franklin Hyde

*Who caroused in the Dirt and was corrected by
His Uncle.*

His Uncle came on Franklin Hyde
Carousing in the Dirt.
He Shook him hard from Side to Side
And Hit him till it Hurt,
Exclaiming, with a Final Thud,
'Take that! Abandoned Boy!
For Playing with Disgusting Mud
As though it were a Toy!'

[101]

Moral

From Franklin Hyde's adventure, learn
To pass your Leisure Time
In Cleanly Merriment, and turn
From Mud and Ooze and Slime
And every form of Nastiness —
But, on the other Hand,
Children in ordinary Dress
May always play with Sand.

HILAIRE BELLOC (1870–1953)

91 Nursery Rules from Nannies

Many little cuss words, bother, dash and blow,
And other little wuss words, can send us down below.

The little boy who would not say 'Thank you' and 'If you
    please',
Was scraped to death with oyster shells among the
    Caribees.

We don't like that girl from Tooting Bec,
She washes her face, and forgets her neck.

92 Reflection on Babies

A bit of talcum
Is always walcum.

OGDEN NASH (1902–70)

93 Lines to be Embroidered on a Bib, Or, The Child is Father of the Man, but Not for Quite a While

So Thomas Edison
Never drank his medicine;
So Blackstone and Hoyle
Refused cod-liver oil;
So Sir Thomas Malory
Never heard of a calory;
So the Earl of Lennox
Murdered Rizzio without the aid of vitamins or
    calisthenox;
So Socrates and Plato
Ate dessert without finishing their potato;
So spinach was too spinachy
For Leonardo da Vinaci;
Well, it's all immaterial,
So eat your nice cereal,
And if you want to name your own ration,
First go get a reputation.

OGDEN NASH (1902–70)

94 Spring and Fall

To a Young Child

Márgarét, áre you gríeving
Over Goldengrove unleaving?
Leáves líke the things of man, you
With your fresh thoughts care for, can you?
Áh! ás the heart grows older
It will come to such sights colder
By and by, nor spare a sigh
Though worlds of wanwood leafmeal lie;
And yet you wíll weep and know why.

Now no matter, child, the name:
Sórrow's spríngs áre the same.
Nor mouth had, no nor mind, expressed
What heart heard of, ghost guessed:
It ís the blight man was born for,
It is Margaret you mourn for.

GERARD MANLEY HOPKINS (1844–89)

9 Useful for Medicine

95 The Benefits and Abuse of Alcohol

Three cups of wine a prudent man may take;
The first of these for constitution's sake;
The second to the girl he loves the best;
The third and last to lull him to his rest,
Then home to bed! but if a fourth he pours,
That is the cup of folly, and not ours;
Loud noisy talking on the fifth attends;
The sixth breeds feuds and falling-out of friends;
Seven beget blows and faces stain'd with gore;
Eight, and the watch-patrole breaks ope the door;
Mad with the ninth, another cup goes round,
And the swill'd sot drops senseless to the ground.

EUBULUS (4th century BC)
From *The Deipnosophists of Athenaeus*
Translated by RICHARD CUMBERLAND
(1732–1811)

96 Hangover Cures

Last evening you were drinking deep,
So now your head aches. Go to sleep;
Take some boiled cabbage when you wake;
And there's an end of your headache.

ALEXIS (C.350 BC)

Instead of cabbage, acorns boil to-morrow,
Which equally rid you of all your sorrow.

NICOCHARES (C.400 BC)

[105]

When one's been drunk, the best relief I know
Is stern misfortune's unexpected blow;
For that at once all languor will dispel,
As sure as cabbage.

AMPHIS (4th century BC)

97 Beware of Figs

But if a man should eat green figs at noon,
And then go off to sleep; immediately
A galloping fever comes on him, accursed,
And falling on him brings up much black bile.

NICOPHON (c.400 BC)
96 and 97 from *The Deipnosophists of Athenaeus*
Translated by CHARLES DUKE YONGE
(1812–91)

98 Traditional Charms for Various Ailments

Hiccups

Hickup, hickup, go away,
Come again another day:
Hickup, hickup, when I bake,
I'll give to you a butter-cake.

[106]

Burns

Two angels from the North,
One brought fire, the other brought frost:
Out fire!
In frost!
In the name of the Father, Son, and Holy Ghost.

Bleeding

In the bloud of Adam death was taken,
In the bloud of Christ it was all to-shaken,
And by the same bloud I doo thee charge
That thou doo runne no longer at large.

Corns

Pray tell your querist if he may
Rely on what the vulgar say,
That when the moon's in her increase,
If corns be cut they'll grow apace;
But if you always do take care
After the full your corns to pare,
They do insensibly decay,
And will in time wear quite away.
If this be true, pray let me know,
And give the reason why 'tis so.

From *British Apollo*, 1708

99 Health Food

An apple a day
Keeps the doctor away.
ANON

100 Infant Diseases and Their Treatment

What Infants suffer when they breed their Teeth,
What causes so much Pain, and often Death,
I'll tell; for while to make their way they gnaw
With latent Teeth, and pierce the tender Jaw,
Sharp Humours enter e'er the Tooth appears,
And the soft Gums incessant grinding tears.
By grinding for the bone they break their way,
But dearly for the Bone the Mouth must pay.
And how unfriendly are, in this, the Skies?
That man, what most he wants, most dearly buys.
For Teeth the Stomach serve, and Life maintain,
And none can have the Tooth, without the Pain.
The suff'ring Infant tells it by his Cries,
His driv'ling Mouth he with his Fingers plies,
He strives to help himself, but strives in vain,
The Nurse's help must ease him of his Pain.
In a Hare's Brain his little Fingers dip,
Or what *Sicilian* Bees from Roses sip.
The raging Gum, the Sweets and Softness sooth,
And white amidst the Red appears the Tooth:
As the white Iv'ry in red Coral shines,
Which wrought with curious Art, the Workman joins.
But if the Pain encreases, wash his Head
With Milk and liquid Sweets of Roses made.
Warm be his Bath, and wrap his Infant Skull,
When well it has been wash'd, in downy Wool.
Yet all your Labour's lost, except you find
His Load discharges, and he's lax behind.

[108]

His Body bound, with liquid Honey loose;
What Thing was ever found of greater Use?
Could Heav'n a better Grant, and Earth produce?
This give him at his Mouth, or else convey
The Physick by a Pipe the other way:
But if there wants of this Celestial Dew,
Then Bete or the Marshmalloe Root will do.
And when the Child at once is weak and loose,
White Poppy Seeds into the Purge infuse.
The Berries of the Myrtle Tree prepare,
Which hates the Cold, and is to *Venus* dear.
These with *Cyperus* steep in Milk, and make
A Drink, and wholsom Draughts the Child will take . . .
    Why should I name how the Posterior Pipe
Is apt the Bounds in weakly Babes to slip?
The Muscles, moisten'd when the Belly's loose,
Their nat'ral Duty to discharge, refuse;
And out the *Anus* hangs, a grievous Pain;
Nor is it easily got in again.
The Body bind, foment it when 'tis out,
And gently with thy Hand replace the Gut.

                    M. SAINT-MARTHE (fl. 1580)
From *Paedotrophiae, or the Art of Bringing up Children*
                              (Book III)
                Translated anonymously, 1718

101 The Process of Conception

Beneath those Parts, where stretching to its bound,
The low *Abdomen* girds the Belly round,
The Shop of Nature lies; a vacant Space
Of small Circumference divides the Place,
Pear-like the Shape: within a *Membrane* spreads
Her various Texture of meandrous Threds;
These draw the Vessels to a pursy State,
And or contract their Substance, or dilate.

[109]

Here Veins, Nerves, Arteries in Pairs declare,
How nobler Parts deserve a double Care;
They from the Mass the Blood and Spirits drain,
That irrigate profuse the thirsty Plain;
The Bottom of the *Womb* 'tis call'd; the Sides are cleft,
By Cells distinguish'd into Right and Left.
'Tis thought that *Females* in the Left prevail,
And that the Right contains the sprightly *Male*.
A Passage here in Form oblong extends,
Where fast compress'd the stiffen'd *Nerve* ascends,
And the warm *Fluid* with concurring *Fluids* blends.
The *Sages* this the Womb's Neck justly name;
Within the hollow of its inward Frame,
Join'd to the Parts a small Protub'rance grows,
Whose rising Lips the deep Recesses close.
For while the *Tiller* all his strength collects,
While Hope anticipates the fair Effects,
The lubricated Parts their Station leave,
And closely to the working Engine cleave;
Each Vessel stretches, and distending wide,
The greedy Womb attracts the glowing Tide,
And either Sex commix'd, the Streams united glide.
But now the Womb relax'd, with pleasing pain
Gently subsides into it self again;
The Seed moves with it, and thus clos'd within,
The tender Drops of Entity begin.
What Joy the Fibres of the Stomach feel,
Long pinch'd with Hunger, at a grateful Meal,
Such tickling Pleasure thro the Womb is sent,
When the first Particles of Life ferment.
This easy Picture of the Parts explains
How frequent Motion no Effect obtains;
The Seed and Pleasure lost in eager Strife;
A useful Lesson to the forward Wife.

CLAUDE QUILLET (1602–61)
From *Callipaedia, or the Art of Getting Beautiful
Children* (Book II)
Published in Latin in Paris, 1656
Translated by GEORGE SEWELL (1688?–1726)

102 The Circulation of the Blood

The salient point, so first is call'd the heart,
Shap'd and suspended with amazing art,
By turns dilated, and by turns comprest,
Expels, and entertains the purple guest.
It sends from out its left contracted side
Into th'arterial tube its vital pride:
Which tube, prolong'd but little from its source,
Parts its wide trunk, and takes a double course;
One channel to the head its way directs,
One to th'inferior limbs its path inflects.
Both smaller by degrees, and smaller grow,
And on the parts, thro' which they branching go,
A thousand secret, subtle pipes bestow.
From which by num'rous convolutions wound,
Wrapt with th'attending nerve, and twisted round,
The complicated knots and kernels rise,
Of various figures, and of various size.
Th'arterial ducts, when thus involv'd, produce
Unnumber'd glands, and of important use.
But after, as they farther progress make,
The appellation of a vein they take.
For tho' th'arterial pipes themselves extend
In smallest branches, yet they never end:
The same continu'd circling channels run
Back to the heart, where first their course begun.
   The heart, as said, from its contractive cave
On the left side, ejects the bounding wave;
Exploded thus, as splitting channels lead,
Upward it springs, or downward is convey'd;
The crimson jets, with force elastic thrown,
Ascend, and climb the mind's imperial throne,
Arterial streams through the soft brain diffuse,
And water all its fields with vital dews:
From this o'erflowing tide the curious brain
Does through its pores the purer spirits strain;

Which to its inmost seats their passage make,
Whence their dark rise th'extended sinews take;
With all their mouths the nerves these spirits drink,
Which through the cells of the fine strainer sink;
These all the channell'd fibres every way
For motion and sensation still convey.
The greatest portion of th'arterial blood,
By the close structure of the parts withstood,
Whose narrow meshes stop the grosser flood,
By apt canals and furrows in the brain,
Which here discharge the office of a vein,
Invert their current, and the heart regain.

SIR RICHARD BLACKMORE (1653–1729)
From *Creation* (Book VI)

103 In Praise of Water-Gruel

I always choose the plainest food
To mend viscidity of blood.
Hail! water-gruel, healing power,
Of easy access to the poor;
Thy help love's confessors implore,
And doctors secretly adore;
To thee I fly, by thee dilute—
Through veins my blood doth quicker shoot,
And by swift currents throws off clean
Prolific particles of spleen.

MATTHEW GREEN (1696–1737)
From *The Spleen*

104 The Advantages of Washing

Let those who from the frozen Arctos reach
Parched Mauritania, or the sultry West,
Or the wide flood that laves rich Indostan,
Plunge thrice a day, and in the tepid wave
Untwist their stubborn pores; that full and free
The evaporation through the softened skin
May bear proportion to the swelling blood.
So may they 'scape the fever's rapid flames;
So feel untainted the hot breath of hell.
With us, the man of no complaint demands
The warm ablution just enough to clear
The sluices of the skin, enough to keep
The body sacred from indecent soil.
Still to be pure, even did it not conduce
(As much it does) to health, were greatly worth
Your daily pains. 'Tis this adorns the rich;
The want of this is poverty's worst woe;
With this external virtue age maintains
A decent grace; without it, youth and charms
Are loathsome. This the venal Graces know;
So doubtless do your wives; for married sires,
As well as lovers, still pretend to taste;
Nor is it less (all prudent wives can tell)
To lose a husband's than a lover's heart.

JOHN ARMSTRONG (1709–79)

105 The Dangers of Sexual Excess

Some to extinguish, others to prevent,
A mad devotion to one dangerous fair,
Court all they meet; in hopes to dissipate
The cares of love amongst an hundred brides.
The event is doubtful: for there are who find

[113]

A cure in this; there are who find it not.
'Tis no relief, alas! it rather galls
The wound, to those who are sincerely sick.
For while from feverish and tumultuous joys
The nerves grow languid and the soul subsides,
The tender fancy smarts with every sting,
And what was love before is madness now.
Is health your care, or luxury your aim,
Be temperate still: when Nature bids, obey;
Her wild impatient sallies bear no curb:
But when the prurient habit of delight,
Or loose imagination, spurs you on
To deeds above your strength, impute it not
To Nature: Nature all compulsion hates.
Ah! let not luxury nor vain renown
Urge you to feats you well might sleep without;
To make what should be a rapture a fatigue,
A tedious task; nor in the wanton arms
Of twining Laïs melt your manhood down.
For from the colliquation of soft joys
How changed you rise! the ghost of what you
        was!
Languid, and melancholy, and gaunt, and wan;
Your veins exhausted, and your nerves unstrung.
Spoiled of its balm and sprightly zest, the blood
Grows vapid phlegm; along the tender nerves
(To each slight impulse tremblingly awake)
A subtle fiend that mimics all the plagues,
Rapid and restless springs from part to part.
The blooming honours of your youth are fallen;
Your vigour pines; your vital powers decay;
Diseases haunt you; and untimely age
Creeps on; unsocial, impotent, and lewd.
Infatuate, impious epicure! to waste
The stores of pleasure, cheerfulness, and health!
Infatuate all who make delight their trade,
And coy perdition every hour pursue.

JOHN ARMSTRONG (1709–79)
104 and 105 from *The Art of Preserving Health*

106 Proverbial Advice on Keeping Healthy

Early to bed and early to rise,
Makes a man healthy, wealthy and wise.

After dinner sit awhile;
After supper walk a mile.

If you wish to live for ever,
You must wash milk from your liver.

He that would live for aye
Must eat sage in May.

Button to chin
Till May be in;
Cast not a clout
Till May be out.

Our fathers, who were wondrous wise,
Did wash their throats before they washed their eyes.

The head and the feet keep warm;
The rest will take no harm.

Use three physicians' skill: first, Dr Quiet,
Then Dr Merriman, and Doctor Diet.

In health, they do abuse
Nature, who Physick use.

107 The Value of Dentistry

Let azure eyes with coral lips unite,
And health's vermillion blend with snowy white;
Let auburn tresses float upon the gale,
And flowery garlands all their sweets exhale;
If once the lips in parting, should display
The teeth discolored or in disarray,
The spell dissolves, and beauty in despair
Beholds her fond pretensions melt in air.

But learn the remedy:—the dentist's skill
Subjects disordered nature to his will:—
As great commanders hear without alarms,
The shouts of battle and the shock of arms,
And, when their troops, in broken ranks, incline
To wild confusion, bring them into line;
So he—the master of the dental art,
Can order, grace, and symmetry impart,
Where anarchy had else sustained alone
The undisputed title to his throne.
                    SOLYMAN BROWN (1790–1865?)

108 Tartar

If sloth or negligence the task forbear
Of making cleanliness a daily care;
If fresh ablution, with the morning sun,
Be quite foreborne or negligently done;
In dark disguise insidious tartar comes,
Incrusts the teeth and irritates the gums,

[116]

Till vile deformity usurps the seat
Where smiles should play and winning graces meet,
And foul disease pollutes the fair domain,
Where health and purity should ever reign.

SOLYMAN BROWN (1790–1865?)

109 Caries

Destructive caries comes with secret stealth
T'avenge the violated laws of health:
Dilapidates the teeth by slow decay,
And bears them all successively away.
So, silent Time, with unresisted power,
Labors at midnight in the lonely tower;
Corrodes the granite in the ivied wall,
And smiles to hear the crumbling atoms fall;—

Till all the mighty structure disappears,
A dream forgot, a tale of other years.
When caries, thus, the solid tooth destroys,
That sullen enemy to mortal joys,
The tooth-ache, supervenes:—detested name,
Most justly damned to everlasting fame!

SOLYMAN BROWN (1790–1865?)

110 Artificial Teeth

Behold the dental artist's bright array
Of magic wonders glittering to the day;—
The white stalactite from the mountain cave;
The branching coral from the ocean wave;
The crystal from the rock; the gem that shines
With decompounded light from Indian mines;

[117]

And alabaster; and that yellow stone
That graces jealous beauty's virgin zone;
The brightest gifts of every varying clime,
Resplendent spoils of nature and of time;—
And see, obedient to his ruling will,
Their forms transmuted by his plastic skill,
Till, as when Cadmus, coveting to reign,
With teeth of dragons sowed the Theban plain,
A marshalled host sprang vigorous from the glade,
In blazoned arms and towering plumes arrayed;
So spring to light, while love her flag unfurls,
A shining panoply of orient pearls.

With aids like these, from nature's store supplied,
And following nature man's unerring guide,
The artist boldly ventures to restore
The dental arch, till, perfect as before,
The teeth in order greet the wondering sight,
A theme of admiration and delight!

SOLYMAN BROWN (1790–1865?)
107–10 from *Dentologia: a Poem on the Diseases of
the Teeth and Their Proper Remedies* (Cantos II, III
and IV)

111 Dietary Advice

If you iron tonic need,
Eat more spinach, beet, and swede;
If your nerves are all awry,
Lettuces and onions try.

ANON

112 The Cranial Nerves

On Old Olympia's Towering Top
A Finn And German Vault And Hop.

(The capital letters give the following sequence of nerves:
Olfactory, Optic, Oculomotor, Trochlear, Trigeminal,
Abducens, Facial, Auditory, Glosspharyngeal, Vagus, Acces-
sory, Hypoglossal.)

ANON

113 Epitaph in a Churchyard at Thetford, in Norfolk

My GRANDMOTHER was buried here;
My COUSIN JANE and TWO UNCLES dear;
My FATHER perished with a *mortification in his thighs*;
My SISTER dropped down dead in the Minories:
But the reason why I'M here interr'd, according to my
   thinking,
Is owing to my good living and hard drinking.
If, therefore, GOOD CHRISTIANS, you wish to live long,
Don't drink too much WINE, BRANDY, GIN, or anything
   strong.

ANON

114 Epitaph—on the Wife of Dr Greenwood

Buried in Southampton Churchyard

O cruel Death! thou hast cut down
The fairest GREEN-WOOD in all this kingdom.
Her virtue and her piety were such,
That really she deserved a Lord or a Judge:

[119]

Yet such was her humility,
That she rather chose me, a Doctor in Divinity;
For which heroic action, join'd to all the rest,
She deserves to be esteemed the Phoenix of her sex;
And like that bird her young she did beget,
That those she left behind might not be disconsolate.
And now, my grief for this good woman is so sore,
That really I can write but four lines more.
For this and for another good woman's sake,
Never let a blister be applied to a lying-in woman's neck,
For in all diseases of the bladder and the womb,
It never fails to bring the patient to the tomb.

DR GREENWOOD fecit

115 Cautionary Limerick

When you think of the hosts without No.
Who are slain by the deadly cuco.,
  It's quite a mistake
  Of such food to partake,
It results in a permanent slo.

ANON

10 Useful for Cooks

116 Proverbial Advice on
Eating and Drinking

Cheese it is a peevish elf,
It digests all things but itself.

After melon
Wine is a felon.

Milke before wine, I would 'twere mine;
Milk taken after, is poison's daughter.

Wine upon beer, I counsel thee;
Beer upon wine, let that be.

117 *From* Gastrology

I write these precepts for immortal Greece,
That round a table delicately spread,
Or three, or four, may sit in choice repast,
Or five at most. Who otherwise shall dine,
Are like a troop marauding for their prey.
ARCHESTRATUS (4th century BC)
Translated by ISAAC D'ISRAELI
(1766–1848)

[121]

118 *From* The Art of Cookery

Far from the parlour have your kitchen plac'd,
Dainties may in their working be disgrac'd.
In private draw your poultry, clean your tripe,
And from your eels their slimy substance wipe.
Let cruel offices be done by night,
For they who like the thing abhor the sight.
   Next, let discretion moderate your cost,
And, when you treat, three courses be the most.
Let never fresh machines your pastry try,
Unless grandees or magistrates are by:
Then you may put a dwarf into a pie.
Or, if you'd fright an alderman and mayor,
Within a pasty lodge a living hare;
Then midst their gravest furs shall mirth arise,
And all the Guild pursue with joyful cries.
   Crowd not your table: let your number be
Not more than seven, and never less than three.

WILLIAM KING (1663–1712)

119 Recipes *from* The Deipnosophists of Athenaeus

Onions

Now if you want an onion, just consider
What great expense it takes to make it good:
You must have cheese, and honey, and
   sesame,
Oil, leeks, and vinegar, and assafoetida,
To dress it up with; for by itself onion
Is bitter and unpleasant to the taste.

PHILEMON (361–263 BC)

Gourds

First cut the gourds in slices, and then run
Threads through their breadth, and dry them in the air;
Then smoke them hanging them above the fire;
So that the slaves may in the winter season
Take a large dish and fill it with the slices,
And feast on them on holidays: meanwhile
Let the cook add all sorts of vegetables,
And throw them seed and all into the dish;
Let them take strings of gherkins fairly wash'd,
And mushrooms, and all sorts of herbs in bunches,
And curly cabbages, and add them too.

NICANDER (2nd century BC)

Hare

Many are the ways and many the recipes
For dressing hares; but this is best of all,
To place before a hungry set of guests,
A slice of roasted meat fresh from the spit,
Hot, season'd only with plain simple salt,
Not too much done. And do not you be vex'd
At seeing blood fresh trickling from the meat,
But eat it eagerly. All other ways
Are quite superfluous, such as when cooks pour
A lot of sticky clammy sauce upon it,
Parings of cheese, and lees, and dregs of oil,
As if they were preparing cat's meat.

ARCHESTRATUS (4th century BC)

Sausage

                    I am making soup,
Putting in well-warm'd fish, and adding to them
Some scarce half-eaten fragments; and the pettitoes
Of a young porker, and his ears; the which I sprinkle
With savoury assafoetida; and then
I make the whole into a well-flavour'd sausage,
A meat most saleable. Then do I add a slice
Of tender tripe; and a snout soak'd in vinegar.
                    AXIONICUS (4th century BC)

A Banquet

First I did take some squills,* and fried them all;
Then a large shark I cut in slices large,
Roasting the middle parts, and the remainder
I boil'd and stuff'd with half-ripe mulberries.
Then I take two large heads of dainty grayling,
And in a large dish place them, adding simply
Herbs, cummin, salt, some water, and some oil.
Then after this I bought a splendid pike,
To boil in pickle with all sorts of herbs.
Avoiding all such roasts as want a spit,
I bought too some fine mullet, and young thrushes,
And put them on the coals just as they were,
Adding a little brine and marjoram.
To these I added cuttle-fish and squills.
A fine dish is the squill when carefully cook'd.
But the rich cuttle-fish is eaten plain,
Though I did stuff them with a rich forced meat
Of almost every kind of herb and flower.
Then there were several dishes of boil'd meats,
And sauce-boats full of oil and vinegar.
Besides all this a conger fine and fat

*Probably shrimps.

I bought, and buried in a fragrant pickle;
Likewise some tench, and clinging to the rocks
Some limpets. All their heads I tore away,
And cover'd them with flour and bread crumbs over,
And then prepared them as I dress'd the squills.
There was a widow'd amia too, a noble
And dainty fish. That did I wrap in fig-leaves,
And soak'd it through with oil, and over all
With swaddling clothes of marjoram did I fold it,
And hid it like a torch beneath the ashes.
With it I took anchovies from Phalerum,
And pour'd on them one cruet full of water.
Then shredding herbs quite fine I add more oil,
More than two cotylae in quantity.
What next? That's all. This sir is what I do,
Not learning from recipes or books of cookery.

SOTADES (4th century BC)

Translated by CHARLES DUKE YONGE (1812–91)

120 Methods of Cooking Trout

Restorative broth of Trouts learne to make:
  Some fry and some stew, and some also bake.
First broyl and then bake, is a rule of good skill,
  And when thou dost fortune a great trout to kill,
Then rost him, and baste first with good claret wine,
  But the calvor'd boyl'd trout will make thee to dine
With dainty contentment, both the hot and the cold,
  And the marrionate Trout I dare to be bold
For a quarter of a year will keep to thy mind,
  If covered close & preserved from wind.
But mark well good brother, what now I doe say,
Sauce made of Anchoves is an excellent way,
  With oysters and lemmon, clove, nutmeg and mace,
  When the brave spotted trout hath been boyl'd apace

With many sweet herbs: for forty years I
  In Ambassadours Kitchins learn'd my cookery,
The French and Italian no better can doe,
  Observe well my rules and you'l say so too.

THOMAS BARKER (fl. 1651)
From *The Art of Angling*

121 A Receipt for Stewing Veal

with Notes by the Author

Take a knuckle of veal;
  You may buy it, or steal.
In a few pieces cut it:
In a stewing-pan put it.
Salt, pepper, and mace,
  Must season this knuckle;
Then what's join'd to a place[1]
  With other herbs muckle;
That which killed king Will;[2]
And what never stands still.[3]
Some sprigs[4] of that bed
Where children are bred,
Which much will you mend, if
Both spinnage and endive,
And lettuce, and beet,
With marygold meet.
Put no water at all;
For it maketh things small,
Which, lest it should happen,
A close cover clap on.
Put this pot of Wood's metal[5]

---

1 Vulgo, salary. 2 Supposed sorrel. 3 This is by
Dr Bentley thought to be time, or thyme. 4 Parsley.
Vide Chamberlayne. 5 Of this composition, see the
works of the Copper-farthing Dean.

[126]

In a hot boiling kettle,
And there let it be
  (Mark the doctrine I teach)
About—let me see—
  Thrice as long as you preach;[6]
So skimming the fat off,
Say grace with your hat off.
O, then! with what rapture
Will it fill dean and chapter!

6 Which we suppose to be near four hours.

JOHN GAY (1685–1732)
(Also attributed to ALEXANDER POPE)

122 Logic

Good wine maketh good blood,
Good blood causeth good humours,
Good humours cause good thoughts,
Good thoughts bring forth good works,
Good works carry a man to heaven;
Ergo, Good wine carrieth a man to heaven.

ANON

123 *From* The Art of Making Puddings
I Hasty Pudding.

Sometimes the frugal matron seems in haste,
  Nor cares to beat her pudding into paste:
Yet milk in proper skillet she will place,
And gently spice it with a blade of mace;
Then set some careful damsel to look to't,
And still to stir away the bishop's-foot;
For, if burnt milk should to the bottom stick,
Like over-heated zeal, 'twould make folks sick.

[127]

Into the milk her flour she gently throws,
As valets now would powder tender beaux:
The liquid forms in hasty mass unite
Forms equally delicious, as they're white,
In shining dish the hasty mass is thrown,
And seems to want no graces but its own.
Yet still the housewife brings in fresh supplies,
To gratify the taste, and please the eyes.
She on the surface lumps of butter lays,
Which, melting with the heat, its beams displays;
From whence it causes, wondrous to behold,
A silver soil bedeck'd with streams of gold!

VIII Oatmeal Pudding

Of oats decorticated take two pound,
And of new milk enough the same to drown;
Of raisins of the sun, ston'd, ounces eight;
Of currants, cleanly pick'd, an equal weight;
Of suet, finely slic'd, an ounce at least;
And six eggs newly taken from the nest:
Season this mixture well with salt and spice;
'Twill make a pudding far exceeding rice;
And you may safely feed on it like farmers,
For the receipt is learned Dr Harmer's.

IX A Sack-posset

From far Barbadoes, on the western main,
Fetch sugar, half a pound; fetch sack, from Spain,
A pint; then fetch, from India's fertile coast,
Nutmeg, the glory of the British toast.

WILLIAM KING (1663–1712)

124 Onyons

Come, follow me by the Smell,
Here's delicate Onyons to sell,
I promise to use you well.
They make the Blood warmer,
You'll feed like a Farmer:
For this is ev'ry Cook's Opinion,
No sav'ry Dish without an Onyon;
But lest your Kissing should be spoyl'd,
Your Onyons must be th'roughly boyl'd;
    Or else you may spare
    Your Mistress a Share,
The Secret will never be known;
    She cannot discover
    The Breath of her Lover,
But think it as sweet as her own.

            JONATHAN SWIFT (1667–1745)

125 Recipe for Salad

To make this condiment, your poet begs
The pounded yellow of two hard-boiled eggs,
Two boiled potatoes, passed through kitchen-sieve,
Smoothness and softness to the salad give;
Let onion atoms lurk within the bowl,
And, scarce suspected, animate the whole.
Of mordant mustard add a single spoon,
Distrust the condiment that bites so soon;
But deem it not, thou man of herbs, a fault,
To add a double quantity of salt.
And, lastly, o'er the flavoured compound toss
A magic soup-spoon of anchovy sauce.
Oh, green and glorious! Oh, herbaceous treat!
'Twould tempt the dying anchorite to eat;

Back to the world he'd turn his fleeting soul,
And plunge his fingers in the salad bowl!
Serenely full, the epicure would say,
Fate cannot harm me, I have dined today.

SYDNEY SMITH (1771–1845)

126 *From* A Ballad of Bouillabaisse

This Bouillabaisse a noble dish is—
    A sort of soup, or broth, or brew,
Or hotchpotch of all sorts of fishes,
    That Greenwich never could outdo;
Green herbs, red peppers, mussels, saffron,
    Soles, onions, garlic, roach, and dace:
All these you eat at Terré's tavern,
    In that one dish of Bouillabaisse.

WILLIAM MAKEPEACE THACKERAY
(1811–63)

127 To Stew a Rump-Steak

Wash it well, and season it hot,
Bind it, and put it in the pot;
Fry three onions, put them to it,
With carrots, turnips, cloves, and suet;
With broth or gravy cover up,
Put in your spoon, and take a sup;
Soft and gentle let it simmer,
Then of port put in a brimmer;
With judgement let the ketchup flow,
Of vinegar a glass bestow;
Simmer again for half an hour,
Serve at six, and then devour.

ANON

128 Recipe for a Pleasant Dinner-Party

A round table, holding eight;
A hearty welcome and little state;
One dish set on a time,
As plain as you please, but always prime;
Beer for asking for—and in pewter;
Servants who don't require a tutor;
Talking guests and dumb-waiters;
Warm plates and hot potaters.

ANON

129 Peas

I eat my peas with honey,
I've done it all my life,
They do taste kind of funny,
But it keeps them on the knife.

ANON

130 Eat with care

Hocus Pocus,
Fish-bones choke us.

ANON

131 Celery

Celery, raw,
Develops the jaw,
But celery, stewed,
Is more quickly chewed.
OGDEN NASH (1902–70)

132 On Tomato
Ketchup

If you do not shake the bottle,
None'll come, and then a lot'll.
ANON

11 Useful for English

133 A Learned Song

Here's A, B, and C,
D, E, F, and G,
H, I, J, K, L, M, N, O, P, Q,
R, S, T, U, V,
W, X, Y, and Z.
And here's the child's dad,
Who is sagacious and discerning,
And knows this is the fount of learning.

Note

This is the most learned ditty in the world: for indeed there is
no song can be made without the aid of this, it being the *gamut*
and groundwork of them all.
Mope's Geography of the Mind.

ANON
From *Mother Goose's Melody*, 1719

134 The Alphabet of Aristotle

A to Amerous, to Adventurous, ne Angre the not to
   moche.
B to Bold, to Besy, and Bourde not to large.
C to Curtes, to Cruel and Care not to sore.
D to Dulle, to Dredefulle, and Drynk not to oft.
E to Ellynge, to Excellent, ne to Ernstfulle neyther.
F to Ferse, ne to Familier, but Frendely of chere.
G to Glad, to Gloryous, and Gelowsy thow hate.

[133]

H to Hasty, to Hardy, ne to Hevy yn thyne herte.
J to Jettyng, to Janglyng, and Jape not to oft.
K to Keping, to Kynd, and ware Knaves tatches among.
L to Lothe, to Lovyng, to Lyberalle of goodes.
M to Medlus, to Mery, but as Maner asketh.
N to Noyous, to Nyce, nor yet to Newefangle.
O to Orpyd, to Ovyrthwarte, and Othes thou hate.
P to Presyng, to Privy, with Princes ne with dukes.
Q to Queynt, to Querelous, to Questife of questions.
R to Ryetous, to Revelyng, ne Rage not to meche.
S to Straunge, ne to Steryng, nor Stare not to brode.
T to Taylous, to Talewyse, for Temperaunce is best.
V to Venemous, to Vengeable, and Wast not to myche.
W to Wyld, to Wrothfulle, and Wade not to depe,
    A mesurabulle meane Way is best for us alle.

> ? MAYSTER BENET, RECTOR OF SANDON, ESSEX
> (15th century)

135 Some Alphabets

A, B, C, D, E, F, G,
H, I, J, K, L, M, N, O, P,
Q, R, S, T, U, and V,
W, X, Y, Z—
Off to bed.

> ANON

Great A was alarmed at B's bad behaviour,
Because C, D, E, F, denied G a favour,
H had a husband with I, J, K, and L,
M married Mary and taught her scholars how to spell;
A, B, C, D, E, F, G, H, I, J, K, L, M, N,
O, P, Q, R, S, T, U, V, W, X, Y, Z.

> ANON

A was an Apple pie, B Bit it, C Cut it,
D Dealt it, E Eat it, F Fought for it,
G Got it, H Had it, I Inspected it,
J Joined for it, K Kept it, L Longed for it.
M Mourned for it, N Nodded at it,
O Opened it, P Peeped in it,
Q Quartered it, R Ran for it, S Stole it,
T Took it, U Upset it, V Viewed it,
W Wanted it,
XYZ All wished for a piece in hand.

(*alternative endings*:
X Y Z and Ampersy-and,
They all wished for a piece in hand.

or X crossed it, Y yearn'd for it, and Z put
    it in his pocket and said, Well done!)

At last they every one agreed
Upon the apple-pye to feed;
But as there seem'd to be so many,
Those who were last might not have any.
Unless some method there was taken,
That every one might save their bacon.
They all agreed to stand in order
Around the apple-pye's fine border.
Take turn as they in hornbook stand,
From great A down to &,
In equal parts the pye divide,
As you may see on t'other side.

ANON

136 A Curious Discourse that Passed between the Twenty-Five Letters at Dinner-Time

Says A, give me a good large slice.
Says B, a little bit, but nice.
Says C, cut me a piece of crust.
Take it, says D, it's dry as dust.
Says E, I'll eat now fast, who will.
Says F, I vow I'll have my fill.
Says G, give it me good and great.
Says H, a little bit I hate.
Says I, I love the juice the best,
And K the very same confest.
Says L, there's nothing more I love,
Says M, it makes your teeth to move.
N noticed what the others said;
O others' plates with grief survey'd.
P praised the cook up to the life.
Q quarrell'd 'cause he'd a bad knife.
Says R, it runs short, I'm afraid.
S silent sat, and nothing said.
T thought that talking might lose time;
U understood it at meals a crime.
W wish'd there had been a quince in;
Says X, those cooks there's no convincing.
Says Y, I'll eat, let others wish.
Z sat as mute as any fish,
While Ampersy-and he licked the dish.

ANON

137 A was an Archer

A was an archer, who shot at a frog;
B was a butcher, and kept a great dog.
C was a captain, all covered with lace;
D was a drunkard, and had a red face.
E was an esquire, with insolent brow;
F was a farmer and followed the plough.
G was a gamester, who had but ill-luck;
H was a hunter, and hunting a buck.
I was an innkeeper, who loved to bouse;
J was a joiner, and built up a house.
K was King William, once governed this land;
L was a lady, who had a white hand.
M was a miser, and hoarded up gold;
N was a nobleman, gallant and bold.
O was an oyster wench, and went about town,
P was a parson, and wore a black gown.
Q was a queen, who was fond of flip;
R was a robber, and wanted a whip.
S was a sailor, and spent all he got;
T was a tinker, and mended a pot.
U was a usurer, a miserable elf;
V was a vintner, who drank all himself.
W was a watchman, and guarded the door;
X was expensive, and so became poor.
Y was a youth, who did not love school;
Z was a zany, a silly old fool.

ANON

138 A Single-Rhyme Alphabet

A was an Army, to settle disputes;
B was a Bull, not the mildest of brutes;
C was a Cheque, duly drawn upon Coutts;

D was King David, with harps and with lutes;
E was an Emperor, hailed with salutes;
F was a Funeral, followed by mutes;
G was a Gallant in Wellington boots;
H was a Hermit, and lived upon roots;
I was Justinian his Institutes;
K was a Keeper, who commonly shoots;
L was a Lemon the sourest of fruits;
M was a Ministry—say Lord Bute's;
N was Nicholson, famous on flutes;
O was an Owl, that hisses and hoots;
P was a Pond, full of leeches and newts;
Q was a Quaker in whitey-brown suits;
R was a Reason, which Paley refutes;
S was a Sergeant with twenty recruits;
T was Ten Tories of doubtful reputes;
U was Uncommonly bad cheroots;
V Vicious motives, which malice imputes;
X an Ex-King driven out by emeutes;
Y is a Yarn; then, the last rhyme that suits,
Z is the Zuyder Zee, dwelt in by coots.

ANON (19th century)
From *Notes and Queries*

139 Dolly's Lesson

Come here, you nigoramus,
    I'm 'shamed to have to 'fess
You don't know any letter
    'Cept just your cookied S.

Now listen and I'll tell you.
    This round hole's name is O
And when you put a tail in
    It makes a Q you know.

[138]

And if it has a front door
  To walk in at, it's C;
Then make a seat to sit on
  Right here, and it is G.

And this tall letter, Dolly,
  It's I and stands for me,
And when I put a hat on
  It makes a cup o' Tea.

And curly I is J, dear,
  And half of B is P,
And E without his slippers on
  Is only F, you see.

You turn A upside downwards
  And people call it V;
And if it's twins like this one
  A W it will be.

Now, Dolly, when you's learnt 'em
  You'll know a great big heap—
'Most much's I—Oh, Dolly,
  I believe you's gone asleep.

ANON
From the *Church Family Newspaper*,
late 19th century

140 On the Vowels—a Riddle

We are little airy creatures,
All of different voice and features:
One of us in glass is set,
One of us you'll find in jet,

T'other you may see in tin,
And the fourth a box within;
If the fifth you should pursue,
It can never fly from you.

JONATHAN SWIFT (1667–1745)

141 I before E

I before E,
Except after C
(Or when it's 'eigh',
As in 'neighbour' or 'weigh').

ANON

142 Principal and Principle

The principal pal of the principal
Is always polite on principle.

ANON

143 Ways of Pronouncing 'Ough'

Though the tough cough and hiccough plough
  me through,
O'er life's dark lough my course I still pursue.

ANON

144 Hints on Pronunciation for Foreigners

I take it you already know
Of tough and bough and cough and dough?
Others may stumble, but not you
On hiccough, thorough, laugh and through?
Well done! And now you wish perhaps
To learn of these familiar traps?

Beware of heard, a dreadful word,
That looks like beard and sounds like bird,
And dead: it's said like bed, not bead,
For Goodness' sake, don't call it deed!
Watch out for meat and great and threat,
They rhyme with suite and straight and debt.

A moth is not a moth in mother
Nor both in bother, broth in brother,
And here is not a match for there,
Nor dear and fear for bear and pear,
And then there's does and rose and lose—
Just look them up: and goose and choose,

And cork and front and word and ward
And font and front and word and sword.
And do and go and thwart and cart—
Come, come, I've hardly made a start!
A dreadful language? Man Alive,
I'd mastered it when I was five!

ANON

145 Grammar-Rules

O Grammar-Rules, O now your virtues show;
So children still read you with awful eyes,
As my young dove may, in your precepts wise,
Her grant to me by her own virtue know:
For late, with heart most high, with eyes most low,
I craved the thing which ever she denies;
She, lightning love, displaying Venus' skies,
Lest once should not be heard, twice said, No, No.
Sing then, my Muse, now *Io Paean* sing;
Heavens, envy not at my high triumphing,
But grammar's force with sweet success confirm:
For grammar says,—O this, dear Stella, say,—
For grammar says,—to grammar who says nay?—
That in one speech two negatives affirm!

SIR PHILIP SIDNEY (1554–86)
From *Astrophel and Stella* (Sonnet LXIII)

146 The Parts of Speech

Three little words you often see
Are ARTICLES, *a*, *an*, and *the*.
A NOUN's the name of anything;
As *school*, or *garden*, *hoop* or *swing*.
ADJECTIVES tell the kind of noun;
As *great*, *small*, *pretty*, *white* or *brown*.
Instead of noun the PRONOUNS stand;
Her head, *his* face, *our* arms, *your* hand.★
VERBS tell of something being done;
To *read*, *count*, *sing*, *laugh*, *jump* or *run*.
How things are done the ADVERBS tell;
As *slowly*, *quickly*, *ill*, or *well*.

★This couplet, being incorrect, is less useful
than the rest of the verse.

CONJUNCTIONS join the words together;
As, men *and* women, wind *or* weather.
The PREPOSITION stands before
A noun, as *in* or *through* a door.
The INTERJECTION shows surprise;
As, *oh*! how pretty! *ah*! how wise!
The whole are called nine parts of speech.
Which reading, writing, speaking teach.

ANON

147 Why English is So Hard

We'll begin with a box, and the plural is boxes;
But the plural of ox should be oxen, not oxes.
Then one fowl is goose, but two are called geese;
Yet the plural of moose should never be meese.
You may find a lone mouse or a whole lot of mice,
But the plural of house is houses, not hice.
If the plural of man is always called men,
Why shouldn't the plural of pan be called pen?
The cow in the plural may be cows or kine,
But the plural of vow is vows, not vine.
And I speak of a foot, and you show me your feet,
But I give you a boot—would a pair be called beet?
If one is a tooth and a whole set are teeth,
Why shouldn't the plural of booth be called beeth?
If the singular is this, and the plural is these,
Should the plural of kiss be nicknamed kese?
Then one may be that, and three may be those,
Yet the plural of hat would never be hose;
We speak of a brother, and also of brethren,
But though we say mother, we never say methren.
The masculine pronouns are he, his, and him,
But imagine the feminine she, shis, and shim!
So our English, I think you will all agree,
Is the trickiest language you ever did see.

ANON

148 Singular Singulars, Peculiar Plurals

How singular some old words are!
I know two with *no* singular:
Agenda, marginalia, both
Are always plural, 'pon my oath.

The opposite's the case to greet us
With *propaganda* and *coitus*;
Upon these never sets the sun,
And yet of each there's only one.
Phantasmagoria, likewise,
Pervades, yet never multiplies.

Strata pluralises *stratum,*
Ultimata, ultimatum;
Memoranda, memorandum;
Candelabra, candelabrum.
Why are *nostrums* then not *nostra*?
Why speak I not then from *rostra*?
Thus my *datum* grows to *data,*
My *erratum* to *errata.*

Child, put this on your next *agendum*:
Pudenda's 'more than one *pudendum*';
Medium makes *media*;
Criterion, criteria;
What's plural for *hysteria*?

WILLARD R. ESPY (b. 1910)

149 What's the Plural?

No one for spelling at a loss is
Who boldly spells Rhinocerosses;
I've known a few (I can't say lots)
Who called the beasts Rhinocerots,
Though they are not so bad (O fie!)
As those who say Rhinoceri.
One I have heard (O holy Moses!)
Who plainly said Rhinoceroses,
While possibly a Fourth-Form Boy
Might venture on Rhinoceroi—
The moral that I draw from these is
The plural's what one damn well pleases.

ANON

150 Memoria Technica for the Plays of Shakespeare

omitting the Historical English Dramas, 'quos versu dicere non est.'

Cymbeline, Tempest, Much Ado, Verona,
Merry Wives, Twelfth Night, As You Like It, Errors,
Shrew Taming, Night's Dream, Measure, Andronicus,
   Timon of Athens.
Wintry Tale, Merchant, Troilus, Lear, Hamlet,
Love's Labour, All's Well, Pericles, Othello,
Romeo, Macbeth, Cleopatra, Caesar, Coriolanus.

ANON

From a Common-place Book at Audley End, reprinted in
Notes and Queries, 1852

151 Principal British Writers

GILDAS a Latin *History of Britain's Conquest* wrote,
CAEDMON, in Anglo-Saxon, a *Paraphrase* of note;
Church History of Angles wrote the Venerable *Bede*;
King ALFRED made *Translations*, which his subjects learned
  to read.
AELFRIC in Saxon wrote, but SCOTUS in the Latin tongue.
WILLIAM and GEOFFREY should be named historians among,
Who flourished in First Henry's reign. Poetic skill we trace
In LAYAMON'S translation of *Brut d'Angleterre*, by WACE.
The works of RALPH DE GLANVILLE to this day do lawyers
  quote:
The *Ormulum* 'mongst early works we must not fail to
  note.

Early English

Piers Plowman's Vision LONGLANDE wrote, of satires not the
  least;
SIR JOHN DE MANDEVILLE describes his *Travels in the East*.
JOHN WICKLIFFE's fame as Lollard and translator never
  fails;
And that of GEOFFREY CHAUCER rests on *Canterbury
Tales*.
John Gower holds a worthy place. JOHN BARBOUR and
  DUNBAR,
King JAMES the First and GAVIN DOUGLAS, Scottish poets
  are.

Middle English

When WILLIAM CAXTON introduced his famous
  PRINTING Press,
He showed its use by publishing *The Game and Playe of
  Chesse*.

[146]

Utopia wrote SIR THOMAS MORE, in reign of Henry Eight;
And WILLIAM TYNDALE's *Bible* is almost equal date.
MILES COVERDALE's soon followed, and in every church
  was chained;
Blank verse to greater purity through SURREY's works
  attained.

Modern English

(Elizabeth's reign)

Sir PHILIP SIDNEY's prose romance *Arcadia* was named;
As author of the *Faerie Queene* is EDMUND SPENSER
  famed.
MARLOWE eight plays, *The Jew of Malta, Faustus* also,
  wrote:
The works of WILLIAM SHAKESPEARE 'twere
  superfluous to quote.
BEAUMONT and FLETCHER wrote in concert two-and-fifty
  plays.
BEN JONSON, ASCHAM, STOW and HOOKER graced these
  palmy days.

DONNE, DRUMMOND, MASSINGER, and BURTON wrote in
  James' reign,
But FRANCIS BACON's learned works to greatest note
  attain.

Chief authors in the troubled reign of the unhappy Charles,
Were ROBERT HERRICK, EDMUND WALLER,
  CHILLINGWORTH, and QUARLES.

Then followed COWLEY, WALTON, TAYLOR, and SIR
  THOMAS BROWNE,
But these to blind JOHN MILTON yield the poet's laurel
  crown.

HYDE, BUTLER, PEPYS also wrote in Charles the Second's
reign;
BAXTER's *Saints' Rest* was published, nor did BUNYAN
write in vain.

JOHN DRYDEN flourished in this reign, and that of
Second James,
Then VANBRUGH, CONGREVE, EVELYN wrote; and LOCKE
our notice claims.

Queen Anne's reign boasts of MATTHEW PRIOR, OTWAY,
BENTLEY, ROWE,
STEELE, ADDISON, SIR ISAAC NEWTON, BURNET
and DEFOE.
Dean SWIFT, JOHN GAY and THOMAS PARNELL also gained
renown;
While of the 'Artificial School' 'twas POPE that bore the
crown.

THOMSON and COLLINS, ALLAN RAMSAY, SHENSTONE,
YOUNG and GRAY,
And DR SAMUEL JOHNSON, wrote in George the
Second's day.
Then RICHARD SAVAGE, HENRY FIELDING, RICHARDSON
and STERNE,
With GOLDSMITH, BUTLER, HUME and SMOLLETT,
reputation earn.

Third George's reign saw CHATTERTON, and famous
ROBERT BURNS,
The author of *John Gilpin*, too, which every schoolboy
learns.
KIRKE WHITE, and BEATTIE, SHELLEY, BYRON, CRABBE,
now lived, and KEATS:
And CAMPBELL's *Mariner of England* many a boy repeats.
Then followed WORDSWORTH, COLERIDGE, and
SOUTHEY of the Lakes;
MOORE writes his *Irish Melodies*, and SCOTT his novels
makes.

LORD CHESTERFIELD and HORACE WALPOLE *Letters* wrote in
  prose;
JAMES BOSWELL's *Life of Doctor Johnson* everybody knows.
Then BRINSLEY SHERIDAN, CHARLES LAMB, and PALEY the
  divine,
With ROBERTSON and GIBBON in the list of authors
  shine.
JAMES MACINTOSH and DUGALD STEWART, BENTHAM too,
  we quote:
In this reign ADAM SMITH and WILLIAM BLACKSTONE
  wrote.

NOON TALFOURD was a dramatist in Fourth King George's
  reign;
Then SHERIDAN KNOWLES and MARRYAT as authors favour
  gain.

HOOD, TENNYSON, and ROBERT BROWNING,
  THACKERAY and HARE,
CHARLES DICKENS, LYTTON, and MACAULAY, all showed
  genius rare.
And names like HALLAM, ALISON, CARLYLE, and STUART
  MILL,
FROUDE, WHATELY, GROTE, and HAMILTON, a brilliant list
  might fill.

                          EDWARD B. GOODWIN (fl. 1875)

152 Metrical Feet

Lesson for a boy

(Begun for Hartley Coleridge in 1806, and then adapted for his brother, Derwent)

Trōchĕe trīps frŏm lōng tŏ shōrt;
From long to long in solemn sort
Slōw Spōndēe stālks; strŏng fōot! yet ill able
Ēvĕr tŏ cōme ŭp wĭth Dāctўl trĭsўllăblĕ.
Ĭambĭcs mārch frŏm shōrt tŏ lōng; —
Wĭth ă lēap ănd ă bōund thĕ swĭft Ānăpăests thrōng;
One syllable long, with one short at each side,
Ămphībrăchўs hāstes wĭth ă stātelў stride; —
Fīrst ănd lāst bēĭng lōng, mīddlĕ shōrt, Ămphĭmācer
Strīkes hĭs thūndērĭng hōofs līke ă prōud hīgh-brĕd Rācer.
If Derwent be innocent, steady, and wise,
And delight in the things of earth, water, and skies;
Tender warmth at his heart, with these metres to show it,
With sound sense in his brains, may make Derwent a
    poet, —
May crown him with fame, and must win him the love
Of his father on earth and his Father above.
    My dear, dear child!
Could you stand upon Skiddaw, you would not from its
    whole ridge
See a man who so loves you as your fond s. t. COLERIDGE

The Homeric Hexameter, described and exemplified

Strongly it bears us along in swelling and limitless billows,
Nothing before and nothing behind but the sky and the
    ocean.

The Ovidian Elegiac Metre, described and exemplified

In the hexameter rises the fountain's silvery column;
In the pentameter aye falling in melody back.

SAMUEL TAYLOR COLERIDGE (1772–1834)

153 From An Essay on Criticism

But most by numbers judge a poet's song:
And smooth or rough, with them, is right or wrong:
In the bright muse, though thousand charms conspire,
Her voice is all these tuneful fools admire;
Who haunts Parnassus but to please the ear,
Not mend their minds; as some to church repair,
Not for the doctrine, but the music there.
These equal syllables alone require,
Though oft the ear the open vowels tire;
While expletives their feeble aid do join;
And ten low words oft creep in one dull line:
While they ring round the same unvaried chimes,
With sure returns of still expected rhymes;
Where'er you find 'the cooling western breeze,'
In the next line, it 'whispers through the trees':
If crystal streams 'with pleasing murmurs creep':
The reader's threaten'd (not in vain) with 'sleep.'
Then, at the last and only couplet fraught
With some unmeaning thing they call a thought,
A needless Alexandrine ends the song,
That, like a wounded snake, drags its slow length along.
Leave such to tune their own dull rhymes, and know
What's roundly smooth, or languishingly slow;
And praise the easy vigour of a line,
Where Denham's strength, and Waller's sweetness join.
True ease in writing comes from art, not chance,
As those move easiest who have learn'd to dance.

'Tis not enough no harshness gives offence,
The sound must seem an echo to the sense:
Soft is the strain when Zephyr gently blows,
And the smooth stream in smoother numbers flows;
But when loud billows lash the sounding shore,
The hoarse, rough verse should like the torrent roar.
When Ajax strives some rock's vast weight to throw,
The line too labours, and the words move slow:
Not so, when swift Camilla scours the plain,
Flies o'er the unbending corn, and skims along the main.

ALEXANDER POPE (1688–1744)

154 On Writing for the Stage

First, then, soliloquies had need be few,
Extremely short, and spoke in passion too.
Our lovers talking to themselves, for want
Of others, make the pit their confidant;
Nor is the matter mended yet, if thus
They trust a friend, only to tell it us;
Th'occasion should as naturally fall,
As when Bellario confesses all.
   Figures of speech, which poets think so fine,
(Art's needless varnish to make Nature shine)
All are but paint upon a beauteous face,
And in descriptions only claim a place:
But, to make rage declaim, and grief discourse,
From lovers in despair fine things to force,
Must needs succeed; for who can choose but pity
A dying hero, miserably witty?
But, oh! the dialogues, where jest and mock
Is held up like a rest at shittle-cock;
Or else, like bells, eternally they chime,
They sigh in simile, and die in rhyme.
What things are these who would be poets thought,
By nature not inspir'd, nor learning taught?

Some wit they have, and therefore may deserve
A better course than this, by which they starve:
But to write plays! why, 'tis a bold pretence
To judgement, breeding, wit, and eloquence:
Nay, more; for they must look within, to find
Those secret turns of nature in the mind:
Without this part, in vain would be the whole,
And but a body all, without a soul.

JOHN SHEFFIELD, 1ST DUKE OF BUCKINGHAM AND
NORMANBY (1648-1721)
From *Essay on Poetry*

155 *From* An Essay on Translated Verse

Each poet with a different talent writes,
One praises, one instructs, another bites.
Horace did ne'er aspire to epic bays,
Nor lofty Maro stoop to lyric lays.
Examine how your humour is inclin'd,
And which the ruling passion of your mind;
Then, seek a poet who your way does bend,
And choose an author as you choose a friend.
United by this sympathetic bond,
You grow familiar, intimate, and fond;
Your thoughts, your words, your styles, your souls agree,
No longer his interpreter, but he.

★ ★ ★

Excursions are inexpiably bad;
And 'tis much safer to leave out than add.
Abstruse and mystic thoughts you must express
With painful care, but seeming easiness;
For Truth shines brightest through the plainest dress.

WENTWORTH DILLON, 4TH EARL OF ROSCOMMON
(1633-85)

[153]

156 To Make a Pastoral: A Receipt

Take *quantum sufficit* of meadows and trees,
While your zephyrs most wantonly play in each breeze;
Let Phoebus and Flora together combine
To make the sky smile and the meadows look fine.
Your nymphs and your swains must be sorted in pairs;
Your swains should be love-sick, your nymphs be all fairs:
Let them prattle awhile, as their hay they are tedding;
Then wind up the whole with a church and a wedding.
But if grief elegiac you'd wish to assail,
Your prospect must lour, your swains must look pale:
Let Damon ask Corydon why droops his head;
If his Celia's unkind, or his lambkins are dead.
'No!' let him reply, ''tis not this gives me pain;
But young Colin is dead, the delight of the plain!'
Then let him invoke skies, angels, and saints,
Trees, meadows, and riv'lets, to join their complaints:
Till Damon, to ease him, and end these sad cries,
Assures him that Colin has mounted the skies.
From this kind assurance his mind is at ease,
And they hie to their cottage—to eat bread and cheese.

ANON
From *Wit's Magazine*, 1787

157 A Familiar Letter

To Several Correspondents

Yes, write, if you want to, there's nothing like trying;
    Who knows what a treasure your casket may hold?
I'll show you that writing's as easy as lying
    If you'll listen to me as the art I unfold.

Here's a book full of words; one can choose as he fancies,
  As a painter his tint, as a workman his tool;
Just think! all the poems, and plays and romances
  Were drawn out of this, like the fish from a pool!

You can wander at will through its syllabled mazes,
  And take all you want,—not a copper they cost,—
What is there to hinder your picking out phrases
  For an epic as clever as 'Paradise Lost?'

Don't mind if the index of sense is at zero,
  Use words that run smoothly, whatever they mean;
Leander and Lilian and Lillibullero
  Are much the same thing in the rhyming machine.

There are words so delicious their sweetness will smother
  That boarding-school flavour of which we're afraid,—
There is 'lush' is a good one, and 'swirl' is another,—
  Put both in one stanza, its fortune is made.

With musical murmurs and rhythmical closes
  You can cheat us of smiles when you've nothing to tell;
You hand us a nosegay of milliner's roses,
  And we cry with delight, 'Oh, how sweet they *do* smell!'

Perhaps you will answer all needful conditions
  For winning the laurels to which you aspire,
By docking the tails of the two prepositions
  I' the style o' the bards you so greatly admire.

As for subjects of verse, they are only too plenty
  For ringing the changes on metrical chimes;
A maiden, a moonbeam, a lover of twenty
  Have filled that great basket with bushels of rhymes.

Let me show you a picture—'tis far from irrelevant—
  By a famous old hand in the arts of design;
'Tis only a photographed sketch of an elephant,—
  The name of the draughtsman was Rembrandt of Rhine.

How easy! no troublesome colours to lay on,
   It can't have fatigued him,—no, not in the least,—
A dash here and there with a hap-hazard crayon,
   And there stands the wrinkle-skinned, baggy-limbed
beast.

Just so with your verse,—'tis as easy as sketching,—
   You can reel off a song without knitting your brow,
As lightly as Rembrandt a drawing or etching;
   It is nothing at all, if you only know how.

Well; imagine you've printed your volume of verses:
   Your forehead is wreathed with the garland of fame,
Your poems the eloquent school-boy rehearses,
   Her album the school-girl presents for your name;

Each morning the post brings you autograph letters;
   You'll answer them promptly,—an hour isn't much
For the honour of sharing a page with your betters,
   With magistrates, members of Congress, and such.

Of course you're delighted to serve on committees
   That come with requests from the country all round;
You would grace the occasion with poems and ditties
   When they've got a new schoolhouse, or poorhouse, or
pound.

With a hymn for the saints and a song for the sinners,
   You go and are welcome wherever you please;
You're a privileged guest at all manner of dinners,
   You've a seat on the platform among the grandees.

At length your mere presence becomes a sensation,
   Your cup of enjoyment is filled to its brim
With the pleasure Horatian of digitmonstration,
   As the whisper runs round of 'That's he!' or 'That's
him!'

But remember, O dealer in phrases sonorous,
  So daintily chosen, so tunefully matched,
Though you soar with the wings of the cherubim o'er us,
  The *ovum* was human from which you were hatched.

No will of your own with its puny compulsion
  Can summon the spirit that quickens the lyre;
It comes, if at all, like the Sibyl's convulsion
  And touches the brain with a finger of fire.

So perhaps, after all, it's as well to be quiet
  If you've nothing you think is worth saying in prose,
As to furnish a meal of their cannibal diet
  To the critics, by publishing, as you propose.

But it's all of no use, and I'm sorry I've written, —
  I shall see your thin volume some day on my shelf;
For the rhyming tarantula surely has bitten,
  And music must cure you, so pipe it yourself.
                    OLIVER WENDELL HOLMES (1809–94)

158 A Caution to Poets

What poets feel not, when they make,
  A pleasure in creating,
The world, in *its* turn, will not take
  Pleasure in contemplating.
        MATTHEW ARNOLD (1822–88)

13 Useful for History

159 *From* Roman History in Rhyme

AENEAS built, in days of yore,
Lavinium on the Latin shore;
And Alba Longa's power was feared
Until the walls of ROME appeared,
By *Romulus* at length upreared.
The tribes that dwelt there first were these:
The Ramnes, Tities, Lucĕres.
When Romulus had left this earth,
Wise *Numa* reigned, of Sabine birth,
Who temples built, and pontiffs chose.
But *Tullus* combated his foes:
Three brothers with three brothers vie—
Horatii, Curiatii.
And *Ancus* made the Ostian port,
Sublician bridge, and many a fort.

                        EDWARD B. GOODWIN (fl. 1875)

160 Useful Dates

William the Conqueror, ten sixty-six,
Played on the Saxons oft-cruel tricks.

Columbus sailed the ocean blue,
In fourteen hundred and ninety-two.

The Spanish Armada met its fate,
In fifteen hundred and eighty-eight.

In sixteen hundred and sixty-six,
London burnt like rotten sticks.

George the Third said with a smile:
'Seventeen-sixty yards in a mile.'*

161 Henry VIII

Bluff Henry the Eighth to six spouses was wedded:
One died, one survived, two divorced, two beheaded.

ANON (c. 1750)

162 The Gunpowder Plot

Remember, remember
The fifth of November,
The Gunpowder Treason and Plot;
I see no reason why gunpowder treason
Should ever be forgot.
A stick and a stake
For George's sake
So please remember the bonfire.
Fifty barrels lay below
To blow old England's overthrow.
With a dark lantern and a lighted match
That's the way old Guy was catch.
Holler, boys, holler; make the bells ring!
Holler, boys, holler; God save the King!

*This is a rare example of a double mnemonic, which gives two unrelated pieces of information—the date of George III's accession and the number of yards in a mile.

A rope! a rope! to hang the Pope,
A slice of cheese to choke him,
A gallon of beer to drink his health
And a jolly good bonfire to roast him.

ANON

(heard in this form at Bedford in 1904)

163 The Kings and Queens of England

Willy, Willy, Harry, Ste,
Harry, Dick, John, Harry Three,
One, Two, Three Neds, Richard Two,
Henry Four, Five, Six—then who?
Edward Four, Five, Dick the Bad,
Harries twain and Ned the Lad,
Mary, Bessie, James the Vain,
Charlie, Charlie, James again.
William and Mary, Anna Gloria,
Four Georges, William, and Victoria.

(Most versions of this popular rhyme agree, more or less, up until Victoria. Thereafter, there seems to be a choice of endings.)

Edward the Seventh, and then
George the Fifth in 1910.
Edward the Eighth did abdicate,
Then George the Sixth did rule the state.

or

Edward the Seventh, George the Fifth,
Edward the Eighth and George the Sixth.

or

Ned Seventh ruled till 1910,
When George the Fifth came in, and then
Ned went when Mrs Simpson beckoned,
Leaving George and Liz the Second.

ANON

164 The Kings and Queens of England

Will., Will., Hen. Steph. Hen. Dick, John Hen., Eddy
  Ned, Edward,
Dicky two, Hen. Hen. Henry, Edward, Ed., Dicky third,
  Hen. Hen.
Sixth Edward, Ma., Bess Jam., first Charles, Charley two,
  two James,
Prince of Orange Will., Mary, Anne, G.G., G. Billy
  Victor.

ANON
From *Notes and Queries*, 1891

165 Lines on Succession of the Kings of England

Began to
Reign

1066	William the Norman conquers England's state;
1087	In his own forest, Rufus meets his fate;
1100	Though elder Robert lives, Henry succeeds;
1135	Stephen usurps the throne, and Albion bleeds;
1154	Great Second Henry bows at Becket's shrine;
1189	Brave Richard's doom'd in foreign bonds to pine;
1199	Perfidious John submits his crown to Rome;
1216	A long and troubled reign's third Henry's doom;
1272	Edward the first, her king to Scotland gives;
1307	Edward the second cruel death receives;
1327	Two captive monarchs grace third Edward's train;
1377	His grandson Richard is depos'd and slain;
1399	Domestic foes, fourth Henry's arms engage;
1413	France feels at Agincourt, fifth Henry's rage;
1422	The sixth good Henry, realms and son must lose;
1461	While the fourth Edward love and fame pursues;

1483	Yet o'er his children's heads, the trembling crown Uncertain hangs, till Richard pulls it down;
1483	Stain'd with their blood, the fell usurper reigns,
1485	Till the seventh Henry, Bosworth's battle gains, Unites the Roses, and dire faction quells;
1509	Henry the eighth both monks and Pope expels;
1547	England laments sixth Edward's short liv'd bloom;
1553	Mary's short reign restores the faith of Rome;
1558	Eliza forms the church and humbles Spain;
1603	The crowns unite in James's peaceful reign;
1625	Charles, by the axe, his errors must atonc;
1649	Cromwell, without the title, mounts the throne;
1660	False power, false pleasure flatter Charles restor'd;
1685	'Gainst James the second, freedom draws her sword;
1688	The sceptre given to William's patriot hand, A bloodless revolution saves the land;
1702	William and Mary dead, Anne mounts the throne;
1714	To her, first George succeeds, Sophia's son;
1727	Next George the second wore his father's crown;
1760	His grandson George now Britain's sceptre sways, Whom God preserve, and bless with length of days.

ANON

Obviously originating from the reign of George III, printed
in *Notes and Queries*, 1852

166 Lines on the Succession of the Kings of England (reversed)

George the Fourth, the son of *Third*, the grandson of the
    Second,
The son of *First*—*Ann's* cousin he, as history has reckoned;
Ann *Mary Second's* sister, either *James the Second's* daughter,
Brother he of *Second Charles*, son of *First Charles* the
    martyr:

[162]

He *James First's* son, the cousin of *Elizabeth* the Queen,
First Mary's sister, sister she of *Edward Sixth* is seen;
Who son of *Henry Eighth* was, he *Henry Seventh's* son,
Cousin of *Richard Third*, from whom he crown and
    kingdom won;
He uncle dread of *Edward Fifth*, the son of *Edward Four*,
The cause of shame and sorrow both to the repentant
    Shore;
The cousin he of *Henry Sixth*, the son of *Henry Five*,
Fourth Henry's son of *Richard Second* cousin, born to strive:
He grandson was of *Edward Third*, of *Edward Second* son,
First Edward's son, *Third Henry's* son, who was the son of
    John,
John brother was of *Richard First*, the son of *Henry Two*,
He *Stephen's* cousin, cousin he of *Henry First*, he who
Of *William Rufus* brother was, the son of him we call
First William, or the Conqueror, who did this realm
    enthrall.

ANON
Printed in *Notes and Queries*, 1852

167 The Chapter of Kings

A Comic Song,
In Doggerel Verse;
Repeatedly sung with Universal Applause by Mr. Dignum,
at the Theatre Royal, Drury Lane;
and written by
MR. COLLINS
Author of the 'Oral and Pictorial Exhibition,' which
bears that Title.

The Romans in England awhile did sway;
The Saxons long after them led the way,
Who tugg'd with the Dane till an overthrow
They met with at last from the Norman bow!
    Yet, barring all pother, the one and the other
    Were all of them Kings in their turn.

[163]

Bold Willie the Conquerer long did reign,
But Rufus, his son, by an arrow was slain;
And Harry the first was a scholar bright,
And Stephy was forced for his crown to fight;
   Yet, barring all pother, the one and the other
   Were all of them Kings in their turn.

Second Henry Plantagnet's name did bear,
And Coeur-de-Lion was his son and heir;
But Magna Charta was gain'd from John,
Which Harry the third put his seal upon.
   Yet, barring all pother, the one and the other
   Were all of them Kings in their turn.

There was Teddy the first like a tyger bold,
Though the second by rebels was bought and sold;
And Teddy the third was his subject's pride,
Though his grandson, Dicky, was popp'd aside.
   Yet, barring all pother, the one and the other
   Were all of them Kings in their turn.

There was Harry the fourth, a warlike wight,
And Harry the fifth like a cock would fight;
Though Henny his son like a chick did pout,
When Teddy his cousin had kick'd him out.
   Yet, barring all pother, the one and the other
   Were all of them Kings in their turn.

Poor Teddy the fifth he was kill'd in bed,
By butchering Dick who was knock'd on the head;
Then Henry the seventh in fame grew big,
And Harry the eighth was as fat as a pig,
   Yet, barring all pother, the one and the other
   Were all of them Kings in their turn.

With Teddy the sixth we had tranquil days,
Though Mary made fire and faggot blaze;
But good Queen Bess was a glorious dame,
And bonny King Jamy from Scotland came,
  Yet, barring all pother, the one and the other
Were all of them Kings in their turn.

Poor Charley the first was a martyr made,
But Charley his son was a comical blade;
And Jemmy the second, when hotly spurr'd,
Ran away, do you see me, from Willy the third.
  Yet barring all pother, the one and the other
Were all of them Kings in their turn.

Queen Anne was victorious by land and sea,
And Georgy the first did with glory sway,
And as Georgy the second has long been dead,
Long life to the Georgy we have in his stead,
  And, may all his son's sons to the end of the chapter,
All come to be Kings in their turn.

JOHN COLLINS (1742–1808)

168 The Royal Line

William I.	The sturdy Conq'ror, politic, severe;
William II.	Light-minded Rufus, dying like the deer;
Henry I.	Beau-clerc, who everything but virtue knew;
Stephen.	Stephen, who graced the lawless sword he drew;
Henry II.	Fine Henry, hapless in his sons and priest;
Richard I.	Richard, the glorious trifler in the East;
John.	John, the mean wretch, tyrant and slave, a liar;
Henry III.	Imbecile Henry, worthy of his sire;

Edward I.	Long-shanks, well nam'd, a great encroacher he;
Edward II.	Edward the minion dying dreadfully;
Edward III.	The splendid veteran, weak in his decline;
Richard II.	Another minion, sure untimely sign;
Henry IV.	Usurping Lancaster, whom wrongs advance;
Henry V.	Harry the Fifth, the tennis-boy of France;
Henry VI.	The beadsman, praying while his Margaret fought;
Edward IV.	Edward, too sensual for a kindly thought;
Edward V.	The little head, that never wore the crown;
Richard III.	Crookback, to nature giving frown for frown;
Henry VII.	Close-hearted Henry, the shrewd carking sire;
Henry VIII.	The British Bluebeard, fat and full of ire;
Edward VI.	The sickly boy, endowing and endow'd;
Mary.	Ill Mary, lighting many a living shroud;
Elizabeth.	The lion-queen, with her stiff muslin mane;
James I.	The shambling pedant, and his minion train;
Charles I.	Weak Charles, the victim of the dawn of right;
Cromwell.	Cromwell, misuser of his home-spun might;
Charles II.	The swarthy scape-grace, all for ease and wit;
James II.	The bigot out of season, forc'd to quit;
William III.	The Dutchman, call'd to see our vessel through;
Anne.	Anna made great by conquering Marlborough;
George I.	George, vulgar soul, a woman-hated name;
George II.	Another, fonder of his fee than fame;
George III.	A third, too weak, instead of strong, to swerve;
George IV.	And fourth, whom Canning and Sir Will preserve.

LEIGH HUNT (1784–1859)

169 *From* English History in Rhyme, or a Rhyming Epitome of the History of England, from B.C. 55 to A.D. 1872

Saxon Period A.D. 450

The growth of HEPTARCHY we trace,
Since Hengist found in *Kent* a place;
For *Sussex* was by Ella gained,
And Cerdic then in *Wessex* reigned;
Ercenwin was in *Essex* crowned;
East Anglia was Uffa's ground;
The *North* to Ida soon gave way;
Then *Mercia* yields to Penda's sway.
Augustine, when by Gregory sent,
Baptized King Ethelbert of Kent.
Egbert the Heptarchy unites;
At Hengesdown the Danes he fights.
The next king *Ethelwulf* was called,
And after him came *Ethelbald*;
Then *Ethelbert* and *Ethelred*.
Great Alfred next, who, it is said,
To Athelney for refuge fled;
As minstrel came to Guthrum's tent,
And then drove Hasting out of Kent.
This king wrote books, translated Bede,
And many useful laws decreed.
Edward the Elder claimed the throne;
Then *Athelstane*, who's better known.
(First) *Edmund*, by an outlaw slain.
St. Dunstan rose in *Edred's* reign.
Next *Edwy* ruled, and *Edgar* too;
Then *Edward*, whom Elfrida slew;
And thus made way for *Ethelred*,
By whom much Danish blood was shed.
Dane-geld he levied; but in vain:
The Unready's throne was seized by Sweyn.
Two kings the sceptre then divide:—
Canute and *Edmund 'Ironside'*.

House of York
Edward IV. 1461

At TOWTON, HEDGELEY MOOR and HEXHAM Edward's
  cause prevailed.
Henry was in the Tower confined. To France Queen
  Margaret sailed.
Edgecot was lost, but Stamford won. Then Warwick
  joined the Queen.
When Edward fled to Holland, on the throne was Henry
  seen.
But Edward, with the Duke of Clarence, won on BARNET'S
  field,
Where Warwick fell. Then Margaret at TEWKESBURY had
  to yield.
Soon Henry died, and Clarence, as 'tis said, in Malmsey
  wine.
Then Edward and King Louis at Pecquigny Treaty sign.
Benevolences Edward raised. A Scottish war took place.
Caxton set up his PRINTING press, and knowledge grew
  apace.

William IV. 1830

Now Louis Philippe became 'King of the French',
And Holland and Belgium asunder they wrench.
In Bristol were riots, 'Reform' was the cry;
Earl Grey became Premier, Lord John his ally,
Who passed the REFORM BILL, though fiercely opposed;
For the Sovereign's consent all resistance soon closed.
The devotion of Wilberforce gratitude craves,
Whose efforts at last secured *freedom to slaves*.
The Poor Laws were mended; Lord Melbourne
  resigned,

But soon replaced Peel, whom the people declined.
Municipal Act was by Brougham promoted.
The Manchester *Railway* great progress denoted.

EDWARD B. GOODWIN (fl. 1875)

170 Presidents of the United States

Washington And Jefferson Made Many A Joke;
Van Buren Had Troubles Plenty To Find.
Pierce Boasted Loud; Johnson Gave Him Good Advice;
Cleveland Hailed Cleveland Made Ruler Twice.

(This mnemonic relies on initial letters to produce the following list:
   Washington, Adams, Jefferson, Madison, Monroe, J. Q. Adams, Jackson, Van Buren, W. H. Harrison, Tyler, Polk, Taylor, Fillimore, Pierce, Buchanan, Lincoln, Johnson, Grant, Hayes, Garfield, Arthur, Cleveland, B. Harrison, Cleveland, McKinley, Roosevelt, Taft.
The awkwardness of the verse suggests that it might be easier just to learn the list.)

ANON (c. 1910)

14 Useful for Latin

171 Memorial Lines on the Gender of Latin Substantives

I General Rules.
The Gender of a Latin Noun
by meaning, form, or use is shown.

1 A Man, a name of People and a Wind,
River and Mountain, Masculine we find:
Rōmulus, Hispānī, Zephyrus, Cōcȳtus,
Olympus.

2 A Woman, Island, Country, Tree,
and City, Feminine we see:
Pēnelopē, Cyprus, Germānia, laurus, Athēnae.

3 To Nouns that cannot be declined
The Neuter Gender is assigned:
Examples fās and nefās give
And the Verb-Noun Infinitive:
Est summum nefās fallere:
Deceit is gross impiety.

List of Prepositions

With Accusative:
Ante, apud, ad, adversus,
Circum, circā, citrā, cis,
Contrā, inter, ergā, extrā,

Īnfrā, intrā, iuxtā, ob,
Penes, pōne, post, and praeter.
Prope, propter, per, secundum,
Suprā, versus, ultrā, trāns;
Add super, subter, sub and in,
When '*motion*' 'tis, not '*state*' they mean.

With Ablative:
Ā, ab, absque, cōram, dē,
Palam, cum, and ex, and ē,
Sine, tenus, prō, and prae:
Add super, subter, sub and in,
When '*state*', not '*motion*', 'tis they mean.
BENJAMIN HALL KENNEDY (1804–89)
From *The Revised Latin Primer*

172 The Declining of a Gallant

SINGULARITER

Nominativo hic gallant asse.
Genitivo hujus brave.
Dativo huic if he get a licke.
Accusativo hunc of a taffaty punck.
Vocativo O he's gone if he cry so.
Ablativo ab hoc he hath got the pock.

PLURALITER

Nominativo hi gallanti, if the pike can defie.
Genitivo horum, yet he is a beggar in *corum*.
Dativo his, his gilt rapier he doth misse.
Accusativo hos, without a cloack he goes.
Vocativo O, woe to the hole he must goe.
Ablativo ab his, thus a gallant declined is.

ANON
From *Wit's Recreations*, 1645

173 Aenigma on the Six Cases

No. *Nanta* was nominated for a W(hore).
Gen. For she that had been *Genitive* before:
Da. Notice hereof was *to the Justice* given,
Acc. *Who her accus'd*, that she had loosely liven.
Voc. But she *cry'd mercy*, and her fault up ript,
Abl. And so was ta'n away and soundly whipt.
   Her Case was ill: yet will the question be,
   Being thus declin'd, in what a case was she.

ANON

From Wit's Recreations, 1645

174 On the Latin Gerunds

When Dido found Aeneas would not come,
She mourn'd in silence, and was Di-do-dum.

RICHARD PORSON (1759–1808)

175 Roman Numerals

   X shall stand for playmates *Ten*;
   V for *Five* stout stalwart men;
   I for *One*, as I'm alive;
   C for *Hundred*, and D for *Five;**
   M for a *Thousand* soldiers true,
   And L for *Fifty*, I'll tell you.

ANON

*i.e. Five Hundred.

176 Aids for Latin

Balls in an over, six you know;
Six INFINITIVES—now let's go.
Present, Perfect, and Future too,
Active, Passive, *three times two*.
Regere, rexisse, recturus esse.
Better to know than to make a guess, eh?
Regi, rectus esse, rectum iri.
Worth learning, e'en though it makes you weary.

PURPOSE CLAUSES are easy to make,
Knowing that *ut* plus Subjunctive they take;
When 'lest' or 'in order that not' is around,
Like horses use *ne* for the negative sound.

GORDON PERRY (b. 1909)

15 Useful for the Sciences

177 What is Liquid

All that doth flow we cannot liquid name,
Or else would fire and water be the same;
But that is liquid which is moist and wet;
Fire that propriety can never get:
Then 'tis not cold that doth the fire put out,
But 'tis the wet that makes it die, no doubt.

MARGARET CAVENDISH, DUCHESS OF
NEWCASTLE (1624–74)

178 A Pint of Water

A Pint of Water
Weighs a Pound and a Quarter.

ANON

179 The Action of Electricity

'Nymphs! your fine hands ethereal floods amass
From the warm cushion, and the whirling glass;
Beard the bright cylinder with golden wire,
And circumfuse the gravitating fire.
Could from each point cerulean lustres gleam,
Or shoot in air the scintillating stream.
So, borne on brazen talons, watch'd of old
The sleepless dragon o'er his fruits of gold;
Bright beam'd his scales, his eye-balls blazed with ire,
And his wide nostrils breath'd inchanted fire.

'You bid gold-leaves, in crystal lantherns held,
Approach attracted, and recede repell'd;
While paper-nymphs instinct with motion rise,
And dancing fauns the admiring Sage surprize.
Or, if on wax some fearless Beauty stand,
And touch the sparkling rod with graceful hand;
Through her fine limbs the mimic lightnings dart,
And flames innocuous eddy round her heart;
O'er her fair brow the kindling lustres glare,
Blue rays diverging from her bristling hair;
While some fond Youth the kiss ethereal sips,
And soft fires issue from their meeting lips.
So round the virgin Saint in silver streams
The holy Halo shoots it's arrowy beams.'

ERASMUS DARWIN (1731-1802)

180 The Action of Invisible Ink

'Thus with Hermetic art the ADEPT combines
The royal acid with cobaltic mines;
Marks with quick pen, in lines unseen portrayed,
The blushing mead, green dell, and dusky glade;
Shades with pellucid clouds the tintless field,
And all the future Group exists conceal'd;
Till waked by fire the dawning tablet glows,
Green springs the herb, the purple floret blows,
Hills, vales, and woods, in bright succession rise,
And all the living landscape charms his eyes.'

ERASMUS DARWIN (1731-1802)
179 and 180 from *The Economy of Vegetation*
(Canto I)

181 Darwin on Species

Hear how selection was the efficient cause
(To form and species of transmuting laws):
There was a time when short-legged, lumbering dogs,
Could only catch the rabbits and the hogs;
The lighter creatures, and the fleeter prey,
Mocked their pursuers as they ran away.
At length the rabbits and the pigs declined,
Till scarce one specimen was left behind;
Then was the breed canine in doleful dumps,
Mourning short commons, and their shorter stumps,
Whilst bounding hares, at which they barked in vain,
Swarmed in the woods, and frolicked on the plain.
At last some turnspits of superior mind
Tried hard the chase, some sustenance to find;
Short-legged, short-winded, much they puffed and blew,
Whilst the fleet game escaped their eager view;
But they, with 'plastic' limbs and watchful care,
In fifty thousand ages caught a hare!
The others died that did not like to run,
Nor was man there to help them with his gun.
Those that remained in time's long cycles found
The way to change a turnspit to a hound;
The sturdy hound, improving on the plan,
Lengthened his legs, and as a greyhound ran:
Thus does *selection's* powers elaborate
Great things from little, little things from great,
To reach the wants of each peculiar state.
In million ages lions grew from cats,
In million ages seals fined down to sprats;
And black bears dabbling in the sea for play,
Lapsed into whales, and grandly swam away.

ANON (mid-19th century)

182 Watt's Improvements to the Steam Engine

His iron-frame, long deem'd so ably plann'd,
Received at first, from Watt's ingenious hand,
A sep'rate cell,* in which the cooling flood
Produced collapses in his vap'rous blood.
Watt, thus apart, secured the end desired,
When heat's full active force was not required;
That in his spacious chest he might insure
A constant, high, and vig'rous temp'rature;
He well foresaw our CHIEF would thus acquire
A vast dilation of his native fire;
Still further this important plan to prove,
His chest, with pond'rous iron-disc above,
Was firmly closed; where erst the cooling damp
Had free access his energy to cramp.
In this great system, with recondite art,
New veinous ducts perform'd their needful part,
And made his blood more freely circulate,
Which moved his limbs at an unwonted rate;
And made at once his new-born vigour gain
As great a force† as iron could sustain.
Nor did he show till that auspicious hour,
Such matchless efforts of continuous power!
     That this prime action, thus so ably gain'd,
Might with full energy be still maintain'd,
The source of all his powers and heart of fire
Self-acting parts for management acquire,
That no excessive, no defective change
Of air‡ or liquids§ might his frame derange,
While heaving pulse, to act in concert made,
To this new process duly gives its aid,
Which from the cooling cell extracts the air,
And tepid water, generated there,

*Watt's new condenser.   †The high pressure principle.
‡The self-acting damper.   §The boiler-feeder.

His power, thus acting 'gainst a perfect void,
Is with full energy at once employ'd.
Meanwhile the liquid, still in tepid state,
Through the whole system made to circulate,
Back to his heart of fire soon finds its way,
Again in vapour's active form to play,
And in his chest its former task repeat,
From thence returning to the source of heat.
As to man's heart the cooling blood returns,
Where life's ethereal flame with vigour burns;
Such is the GREAT CREATOR's glorious plan
Of veinous action in the frame of man!

THOMAS BAKER (?–1871)

183 Means of Propulsion for Steam-Ships

Various devices great mechanics gave
T'impart his action to the crested wave:
The old plane paddles, still in common use,
Some thought the utmost power could not produce;
Divided ones, by some, were next devised;
While the cycloidal were by others prized;
Their curve, so thought the scientific grave,
Conform'd the best to ocean's heaving wave;
And Morgan's novel paddles, too, were tried;
But these and those alike were thrown aside:
For when to Barlow all these schemes were shown,
By his experiments he soon made known,
As well as by Mathesis' rigid test,
That old plane paddles were by far the best:
But Paucton's snake-like screw, behind the car,
The best propeller for the CHIEFS OF WAR,
Is safely placed beneath the rolling sea,
And thus preserved from scaith of gun-shot free.

Rennie's conoidal triple-bladed screw
Displaced the last, and full attention drew;
Ericsson, of aërial-engine fame,
For his six-bladed one advanced his claim;
Three schemes of hope 'twas his to noise abroad,
And all, alas, have gone perdition's road!
While Seguin, Foulton, Cartwright, Shorter, Burns,
Their screws of various forms produced in turns;
Each push'd his project with the wonted zeal
Which all inventors are well known to feel.
But MAUDSLEY'S FEATHERING SCREW of
    double blade
Threw these, and all the rest, into the shade.

THOMAS BAKER (?–1871)

184 The Electric Telegraph

The next grand adjunct to our HERO's cause,
That claim'd at once unanimous applause,
Was Wheatstone's Telegraph, (the Semaphore
By this was number'd 'mong the things of yore,)
This modern prodigy transports the mail
Unseen by human eye o'er hill and vale;
Th'Electric current from Voltaic pyre,
Impetuous urged along th'extended wire,
Deflects the magnet, varied signs displays,
That thus man's thoughts a thousand miles conveys,
With speed at par with th'ethereal light,
Uncheck'd by tempests or the glooms of night!
Nor do meanwhile its needful signals fail,
At every station on th'extended rail,
To point out dangers threat'ning near or far
The glorious march of STEAM's triumphal car.
But now th'admired Electro-type of Bain
Imparts the signs so rapidly and plain,

That thence is read the express from distant climes,
With the same ease as you would read the 'Times!'
Thus train'd, the light'ning gives essential aid
To Britain's state-affairs, her arts and trade,
And guards with arm of superhuman might
This favour'd land of liberty and light.

THOMAS BAKER (?–1871)
182–4 from *The Steam Engine, or the Power of Flame* (Cantos III, VII and X)

185 Facts

Were I to take an iron gun,
And fire it off towards the sun;
I grant 'twould reach its mark at last,
But not till many years had passed.

But should that bullet change its force,
And to the planets take its course;
'Twould *never* reach the *nearest* star,
Because it is so *very* far.

LEWIS CARROLL (1832–98)
(written c.1845)

186 The Copernican System

The Sun revolving on his axis turns,
And with creative fire intensely burns;
Impell'd the forcive air, our Earth supreme,
Rolls with the planets round the solar gleam;

First Mercury completes his transient year,
Glowing, refulgent, with reflected glare;
Bright Venus occupies a wider way,
The early harbinger of night and day;
More distant still our globe terraqueous turns,
Nor chills intense, nor fiercely heated burns;
Around her rolls the lunar orb of light,
Trailing her silver glories through the night:
On the Earth's orbit see the various signs,
Mark where the Sun, our year completing, shines;
First the bright Ram his languid ray improves;
Next glaring wat'ry thro' the Bull he moves;
The am'rous Twins admit his genial ray;
Now burning, thro' the Crab he takes his way;
The Lion, flaming, bears the solar power;
The Virgin faints beneath the sultry shower.
    Now the just Balance weighs his equal force,
The slimy Serpent swelters in his course;
The sabled Archer clouds his languid face;
The Goat, with tempests, urges on his race;
Now in the water his faint beams appear,
And the cold Fishes end the circling year.
Beyond our globe the sanguine Mars displays
A strong reflection of primeval rays;
Next belted Jupiter far distant gleams,
Scarcely enlight'ned with the solar beams;
With four unfix'd receptacles of light,
He tours majestic thro' the spacious height:
But farther yet the tardy Saturn lags,
And five attendant luminaries drags;
Investing with a double ring his pace,
He circles thro' immensity of space.
    These are thy wond'rous works, first Source of good!
Now more admir'd in being understood.

THOMAS CHATTERTON (1752–70)

187 Gemini Jones

At several times the speed of light,
Astronaut Gemini Jones took flight,
Buzzing about, now to, now from,
All the constellations of God's kingDOM:

Ácrux, Ras Álgethis, Tarf, Acanár;
Bénetnasch, Kítalpha, Salm, Giansár;
Cástor, Hercúlis, Skat, Úrsae Majóris,
Délta, Kids, Ádib, Cor, Ursae Minóris;
Eléctra, Dracónis, Poláris, Mizár;
Fúrud, Austrális, Pleióne, Dog Star;
Goméisa, Ed Ásich, Schedár, Sulafát,
Hámal, Kaus Australis, Aldhafera, Skat;
Izár, Sagítirri, Spicá, and Merópe;
Júga, Giánsar, Homám, Asterópe;
Kitálpha, Mekbúda, Yed Pósterior,
Lesáth, Vinddemistrix, Zaurák, Yed Priór;
Mintáka, Porríma, Rasálas, Wasát,
Nashiri, Presépe, Taygéte, Andrát;
Oriónis, Alcyóne, Pegási, Alyá,
Pherkád, Nair al Zúrak, Al Chiba, Alschá;
Rastában, Suzlócin, Canópis, Mwnkár,
Segínis, Algénib, Alphécca, Schedár;
Talítha, Taygéte, Ruchbáh, Scheat, Kocháb,
Unúk al H, Piscium, Altair, Arkáb;
Véga, Peiádum, Graffiés, Leónis,
Wézen, Tarízed, Virgínis, Dracónis;
Yildun, Angeténar, Kaus Boreális,
Záurak, Antáres, Alúla Austrális:

Buzzing about, now to, now from,
All the constellations in God's kingDOM.
                    WILLARD R. ESPY (b. 1910)

188 The Elements

(To be sung to the tune of 'A Modern Major-General')

There's antimony, arsenic, aluminium, selenium
And hydrogen and oxygen and nitrogen and rhenium
And nickel, neodymium, neptunium, germanium
And iron, americium, ruthenium, uranium
Europium, zirconium, lutetium, vanadium
And lanthanum and osmium and astatine and radium
And gold and protactinium and indium and gallium
And iodine and thorium and thulium and thallium.
There's yttrium, ytterbium, actinium, rubidium,
And boron, gadolinium, niobium, iridium
And strontium and silicon and silver and samarium
And bismuth, bromine, lithium, beryllium and barium.

There's holmium, and helium and hafnium and erbium
And phosphorus and francium and fluorine and terbium
And manganese and mercury, molybdenum, magnesium
Dysprosium and scandium and cerium and cesium
And lead, praseodymium and platinum, plutonium
Palladium, promethium, potassium, polonium
And tantalum, technetium, titanium, tellurium
And cadmium and calcium and chromium and curium.
There's sulfur, californium, and fermium, berkelium
And also mendelevium, einsteinium, nobelium
And argon, krypton, neon, radon, xenon, zinc and
    rhodium
And chlorine, carbon, cobalt, copper, tungsten, tin and
    sodium.

These are the only ones of which the news has come to
    Harvard
And there may be many others, but they haven't been
    discarvard.

                          TOM LEHRER (b. 1928)

189 Stalagmites and Stalactites

The mites go up
And the tites come down.

ANON

190 First and Second Law

The First Law of Thermodynamics:
Heat is Work and Work is Heat.

The Second Law of Thermodynamics:
Heat cannot of itself pass from one body to a hotter body.

Heat won't pass from a cooler to a hotter.
You can try it if you like, but you'd far better notta.
Thus the cold in the cooler
Will get hotter as a rule-a,
Because the hotter body's heat will pass to the cooler.

Heat is Work and Work is Heat
And Work is Heat and Heat is Work.

Heat will pass by Conduction;
Heat will pass by Convection;
Heat will pass by Ra-diation;
And that's a physical law.

Heat is Work and Work's a curse
And all the Heat in the universe
'S gonna c-o-o-l down;
'Cause it can't increase.
Then there'll be no more work
And there'll be perfect peace.

Really?

Yeah, that's entropy, man.

And all because of the Second Law of Thermodynamics
That lays down . . .
That you can't pass heat from a cooler to a hotter.
You can try if you like, but you'd far better notta,
'Cause the cold in the cooler
Will get hotter as a rule-a,
'Cause the hotter body's heat will-a pass to the cooler,
And that's a physical law.

Oh, I'm hot.

Hot? That's because you've been Working.

That's the First and Second Law of Thermodynamics.

MICHAEL FLANDERS (1922-75)

16 Useful for Mathematics

191 A Mathematical Problem

To the Rev. George Coleridge

Dear Brother,
    I have often been surprised that Mathematics,
the quintessence of Truth, should have found admirers so
few and so languid. Frequent consideration and minute
scrutiny have at length unravelled the cause; viz. that
though Reason is feasted, Imagination is starved; whilst
Reason is luxuriating in its proper Paradise, Imagination
is wearily travelling on a dreary desert. To assist Reason
by the stimulus of Imagination is the design of the
following production. In the execution of it much may
be objectionable. The verse (particularly in the
introduction of the ode) may be accused of
unwarrantable liberties, but they are liberties equally
homogeneal with the exactness of Mathematical
disquisition, and the boldness of Pindaric daring. I have
three strong champions to defend me against the attacks
of Criticism: the Novelty, the Difficulty, and the Utility
of the work. I may justly plume myself that I first have
drawn the nymph Mathesis from the visionary caves of
abstracted idea, and caused her to unite with Harmony.
The first-born of this Union I now present to you; with
interested motives indeed—as I expect to receive in
return the more valuable offspring of your Muse.
        Thine ever,
        s.t.c.

(*Christ's Hospital*)   *March 31, 1791*

    This is now—this was erst,
Proposition the first—and Problem the first.

I

On a given finite line
Which must no way incline;
To describe an equi-
-lateral Tri-
A,N,G,L,E.
Now let A.B.
Be the given line
Which must no way incline;
The great Mathematician
Makes this Requisition,
That we describe an Equi-
-lateral Tri-
-angle on it:
Aid us, Reason—aid us, Wit!

II

From the centre A. at the distance A.B.
Describe the circle B.C.D.
At the distance B.A. from B. the centre
The round A.C.E. to describe boldly venture.
(Third postulate see.)
And from the point C.
In which the circles make a pother
Cutting and slashing one another,
Bid the straight lines a journeying go.
C.A.C.B. those lines will show.
To the points, which by A.B. are reckon'd,
And postulate the second
For Authority ye know.
A.B.C.
Triumphant shall be
An Equilateral Triangle,
Not Peter Pindar carp, nor Zoilus can wrangle.

III

Because the point A. is the centre
Of the circular B.C.D.
And because the point B. is the centre

Of the circular A.C.E.
A.C. to A.B. and B.C. to B.A.
Harmoniously equal for ever must stay;
   Then C.A. and B.C.
   Both extend the kind hand
   To the basis, A.B.
Unambitiously join'd in Equality's Band.
But to the same powers, when two powers are equal,
   My mind forbodes the sequel;
My mind does some celestial impulse teach,
   And equalises each to each.
Thus C.A. with B.C. strikes the same sure alliance,
That C.A. and B.C. had with A.B. before;
      And in mutual affiance
         None attempting to soar
         Above another,
      The unanimous three
   C.A. and B.C. and A.B.
All are equal, each to his brother,
   Preserving the balance of power so true:
Ah! the like would the proud Autocratix* do!
At taxes impending not Britain would tremble,
Nor Prussia struggle her fear to dissemble;
      Nor the Mah'met-sprung Wight
      The great Mussulman
      Would stain his Divan
With Urine the soft-flowing daughter of Fright.

IV

But rein your stallion in, too daring Nine!
Should Empires bloat the scientific line?
Or with dishevell'd hair all madly do ye run
For transport that your task is done?
   For done it is—the cause is tried!
   And Proposition, gentle Maid,
Who soothly ask'd stern Demonstration's aid,

*The Empress of Russia.

[188]

Has proved her right, and A.B.C.
Of Angles three
Is shown to be of equal side;
And now our weary steed to rest in fine,
'Tis rais'd upon A.B. the straight, the given line.
SAMUEL TAYLOR COLERIDGE (1772–1834)

192 The Value of π

How I wish I
Could calculate pie.

(This mnemonic is based on the number of letters in each of its words. By placing a decimal point after 'How' and allowing a tactical misspelling of 'pi' as 'pie', one achieves the value of π to six places of decimals—3.141593.)

ANON

193 New Maths

You can't take three from two, two is less than three,
So you look at the four in the tens place.
Now that's really four tens, so you make it three tens,
Regroup, and you change a ten to ten ones
and you add them to the two and get twelve
and you take away three, that's nine.

Now instead of four in the tens place
You've got three 'cause you added one
That is to say ten, to the two,
But you can't take seven from the three,
So you look in the hundreds place.

[189]

From the three you then use one to make tens,
And you know why four plus minus one plus ten
Is fourteen minus one?
Because addition is commutative
Right . . .

So now you've got thirteen tens
And you take away seven and that leaves five . . .
Well six actually, but the idea is the important thing.
Now you go back to the hundreds place,
You're left with two and you take away one from two
And that leaves one!

Hooray for New Maths
New Maths!
It won't do you a bit of good to review maths.
It's so simple, so very simple
That only a child can do it.

Now that is actually not the answer that I had in
mind, because the book that I got this problem out
of wants you to do it in base eight. But
don't panic, base eight is just like base ten, really,
if you're missing two fingers.
Shall we have a go at it?

You can't take three from two, two is less than three
So you look at the four in the eights place,
Now that's really four eights, so you make it three eights,
Regroup, and you change an eight to eight ones
and you add 'em to the two
and you get one-two base eight
Which is ten base ten
And you take away three, that's seven.

Now instead of four in the eights place
You've got three 'cause you added one
That is to say eight, to the two,
But you can't take seven from three
So you look at the sixty-fours.

From the three you then use one to make eight eights
And you add those eights to the three
And you get one-three base eight.
Or in other words, in base ten you have eleven
and you take away seven,
And seven from eleven is four.

Now go back to the sixty-fours,
You're left with two.
And you take away one from two
And that leaves one!

Hooray for New Maths
New Maths!
It won't do you a bit of good to review maths
It's so simple, so very simple
That only a child can do it!

                                    TOM LEHRER (b. 1928)

194 Rhymed Mnemonic of the Forty Counties of England

(A New Statesman *Competition Winner)*

Lying south of sweet Northumber
Lands of Westmor, Rut and Cumber,
Nottingham for forest walks,
Durham, Derby, Lancs and Yorks,
Leicester, Warwick, Wilts ahead,
Fords of Here, Staff and Bed,
Shires of Lincoln, Shrop and Ches,
Sexes—Middle, Sus and Es!
Worcester, Gloucester, down the Severn
South to Somerset and Devon,
On to Dorset, Kent and Surrey
Passing London in a hurry.
Berkshire Thames where Oxford punts,
Herts or Bucks for Cambridge Hunts,
Hants and Northants, Norfolk, Suff,
Cornwall, Monmouth—that's enough.

DONALD MONAT (fl. 1959)

195 The Cinque Ports

Dover, Sandwich, and Winchelsea,
Rumney and Rye, the five ports be.

ANON

196 Cornishmen

By Tre, Pol and Pen,
You shall know the Cornishmen.

ANON

197 On the American Rivers

In England rivers all are males—
    For instance, Father Thames—
Whoever in Columbia sails
    Finds them ma'amselles or dames.

Yes, there the softer sex presides,
    Aquatic, I assure ye,
And Mrs. Sippy rolls her tides
    Responsive to Miss Souri.

JAMES SMITH (1775–1839)

198 The Great Lakes of Canada

What about each Great Canadian Lake?
Remembering them is a nice piece of cake;
For they're HOMES for fishes as well as the sea.
H-O-M-E-S is the 5-letter key.

(The initial letters of the lakes are in the acronym HOMES,
giving the following list:
    Huron, Ontario, Michigan, Erie, Superior.)

GORDON PERRY (b. 1909)

18 Useful for Religious Knowledge

199 Memoria Technica for the Books of the Bible
arranged in the order in which they occur

Genesis, Exo, Levi, Num, Deutero, Joshua, Judges,
Ruth, Sam, Sam, King, King, Chron, Chron, Ezra,
   Nehemiah,
Esther, Job, Psalmae, Prov, Eccles, Song Solomonis,
Isaiah, Jeremiah, Lament, Ezekiel, Danielque,
Hosea, Joel, Amos, Obadiah, Jonah, Micah, Nahum,
Habbakuk, Zephaniah, Haggai, Zachariah, Malachi,
Matthaeus, Marcus, Lucas, John, Acts of Apostles,
Rom, Cor, Cor, Gal, Ephes, Phi, Co, Thess, Timothy,
   Tim, Tit,
Phil, Heb, James, Pet, Pet, John, John, John, Jude,
   Revelations.

Apocrypha

Esdras, Esdra, Tobit, Judith, Esth, Wisd, Ecclesiastes,
Bar, Song, Susan, Idol, Manasses, Maccabe, Maccab.

(The above appeared in *Notes and Queries*, 1852, with the following introduction:
'The doggerel Latin hexameters subjoined were made by a Christmas party at Billingbear, eighty years ago. Amongst the contributors I can only point out the names of my father and Sir Thomas Frankland, the sixth baronet, who printed the verses for distribution among his friends. I have often found them useful, and they may be perhaps of service to others.

BRAYBROOKE.')

200 The New Testament

Matthew, Mark, Luke, and John,
The Book of Acts then think upon,
Romans, Cor., remember ye,
Gal., Eph., Phi., Col., three T.s, P.,
Hebrews, James, Peter, and John,
Jude and Revelation.

ANON

201 *From* A Metrical Index to the Bible

*(Which contrives to get the whole Bible into sixty-nine small pages of
verse)*

Genesis

Chap.

1   All things created, Moses writes,
2   And Paradise displays;
3   Tells Adam's fall, which ruin'd all:
4   Cain righteous Abel slays.

5   Before the flood man's life was long:
6   Noah the ark doth frame:
7   The world is drown'd, eight favour found,
8   Out of the ark they came.

9   Cov'nant of rain-bow; Noah drunk,
10   His offspring is increast;
11   They Babel rear, confounded are.
12   Abram is call'd and blest.

13   Departs from Lot: again is blest,
14   'Gainst four kings doth prevail;

[195]

15 A numerous seed is promised,
16   Hagar bears Ishmael.
17 Each male of Abram circumcis'd,
18   He angels entertains:
19 Sees Sodom's flame God's wrath proclaim,
20   His wife his sister feigns.

21 Feasting and mirth for Isaac's birth;
22   He's offer'd, yet spared life:
23 Macphelah's cave, is Sarah's grave,
24   Rebeckah's Isaac's wife.

25 Good Abraham's death, Rebeckah's twins,
26   Isaac his wife denies:
27 Jacob by wiles Isaac beguiles,
28   To Padan-Aram flies.

29 He Rachel weds, and Leah beds,
30   Grows rich by cunning slight:
31 Doth Leban leave, without his leave,
32   Wrestleth with God all night.

33 Jacob and Esau friendly meet,
34   Fair Dinah's foul disgrace:
35 Benjamin's birth is Rachel's death,
36   The dukes of Esau's race.

37 Kept Joseph's in a pit and sold,
38   To Jude twins Tamar bears:
39 Joseph the chaste in prison cast,
40   Two servants' dreams declares.

41 Lights Pharoah's dreams, and is advanc'd,
42   He claps his brethren up;
43 Them, come again, doth entertain:
44   But stops them with his cup.

45 Makes himself known; for Jacob sends,
46   He with his house comes down;

47 In Goshen has a dwelling place,
48   Makes Joseph's sons his own.
49 Next blesseth all his sons, and dies;
50   To Canaan is convey'd:
     And thus, in this book, Genesis,
      You fifty chapters read.

II Thessalonians

Chap.

1 Again their faith and patience prais'd;
2 The Antichrist reveals.
3 Bids them to flee ill company,
4 And then his letter seals.

JOSIAH CHORLEY (?–1719?)

202 The Ten Commandments

Have thou no other gods but me.
Unto no image bow thy knee.
Take not the name of God in vain.
Do not the Sabbath-day profane.
Honour thy father, mother too.
Take heed that thou no murder do.
From whoredom keep thy body clean.
Steal not, although thy state be mean.
Bear not false witness, shun that blot.
What is thy neighbour's covet not.

★ ★ ★

These sacred words, in these ten lines,
Are strings of pearls and golden mines:
Or heaven transcrib'd, wherein, no doubt,
God's mind to man was copied out.

[197]

Bless God, my soul, that thus hath given,
In this thy pilgrimage to heaven,
Such light and guidance: but withal,
Bless God for Christ, that kept them all.

ANON

Published in the 1818 edition of Josiah
Chorley's *A Metrical Index to the Bible*

203 The Lord's Prayer in Verse

Almighty father! of high Heaven possess'd!
Be thy *name* holy, and thy *power* confess'd!
Teach us, on *earth* to know, and do thy *will*;
As *Heaven's* bright train thy great *commands* fulfil.
Gracious, our daily bread of life, bestow:
And show us *mercy*, as we *mercy* show:
Guard us, from strong *temptation's* powerful call;
Nor, when we meet with *evil*, let us fall.

AARON HILL (1685–1750)

204 *From* The Old Testament

Joshua the son of Nun
And Caleb the son of Jephunneh
Were the only two that ever got through
To the land of milk and honey.

ANON

205 *From* A Metrical Version of the Bible, Said to Have Been Composed by a Negro Christian in the State of Massachusetts, and Published in Louisville, Kentucky, in 1858

Adam was de first man and Eve was de *udder*,
Cain was a wicked man for he kill'd his *brudder*.
De *Dibbel* tempted Eve, the apple red to pluck,
She gave one to Adam, who eat it, worse de luck;
Out of Eden he was kick'd, never there *'gen* to return,
De serpent had his legs cut off and crawls now like a worm.

★ ★ ★

David was a shepherd lad, sheep tended night and day,
A lion and a bear did come some sheep to steal away,
But David took a mighty club and both of them did slay.
Goliath, high, did Saul defy, across the river's bed,
But, from the brook, stone David took, and slung it at his
    head,
It struck him low, and with one blow de giant was kill'd
    dead;
When this was done, de foes did run, from Israel they fled.
De Book Divine says Philistine, that day, did die by score,
David alone, with sling and stone, ten thousand kill'd or
    more.

ANON

206 A Model Sermon

It should be brief; if lengthy, it will steep
Our hearts in apathy, our eyes in sleep;
The dull will yawn, the chapel-lounger doze,
Attention flag, and memory's portals close.

It should be warm; a living altar coal,
To melt the icy heart and charm the soul;
A sapless, dull harangue, however read,
Will never rouse the soul, or raise the dead.

It should be simple, practical, and clear;
No fine-spun theory to please the ear;
No curious lay to tickle letter'd pride,
And leave the poor and plain unedified.

It should be tender and affectionate,
As his warm theme who wept lost Salem's fate;
The fiery laws, with words of love allay'd;
Will sweetly warm and awfully persuade.

It should be manly, just, and rational,
Wisely conceived, and well express'd withal;
Not stuff'd with silly notions, apt to stain
A sacred desk, and show a muddy brain.

It should possess a well-adapted grace,
To situation, audience, time, and place;
A sermon form'd for scholars, statesmen, lords,
With peasants and mechanics ill accords.

It should with evangelic beauties bloom,
Like Paul's at Corinth, Athens, or at Rome;
While some Epictetus or Sterne esteem,
A gracious Saviour is the Gospel theme!

It should be mix'd with many an ardent prayer,
To reach the heart, and fix and fasten there;
When God and man are mutually address'd
God grants a blessing, man is truly bless'd.

It should be closely, well applied at last,
To make the moral nail securely fast:
Thou art the man, and thou alone will make
A Felix tremble and a David quake!

ANON

19 Useful for Financiers

207 Proverbial Advice on the Conduct of Business

He that will thrive must rise at five;
He that hath thriven may lie till seven.

Ken when to spend and when to spare,
And when to buy, and you'll ne'er be bare.

Make every bargain clear and plain
That none may afterwards complain.

208 How to Keep Accounts

Receive before you write, and write before you pay,
By strict observance of this rule, keep good accounts
    you may.

ANON

209 Financial Wisdom

You've got to speculate
To accumulate.

ANON

210 Stock Exchange Wisdom

Sell in May
And go away.
ANON

211 Advertisement

The codfish lays a million eggs,
The helpful hen lays one.
The codfish makes no fuss of its achievement,
The hen boasts what she's done.
We forget the gentle codfish,
The hen we eulogise;
Which teaches us this lesson that—
It pays to advertise!

ANON

212 Saffold's Cures

Dear Friends, let your Disease be what God will,
Pray to him for a Cure, try Saffold's Skill;
Who may be such a healing Instrument,
As will cure you to your own Heart's Content.
His Medicines are cheap and truly good.
Being full as safe as your daily Food—
Saffold he can do what may be done, by
Either Physick or true Astrology.
His best Pills, rare Elixir and Powder,
Do each Day praise him louder and louder.
Dear Countrymen, I pray be you so wise
When Men backbite him, believe not their Lies,
But go, see him, and believe your own Eyes.
Than he will say you are honest and kind.
Try before you judge and speak as you find.

THOMAS SAFFOLD? (?– 1691)

213 To Saffold's Customers

At the Golden Ball and Lillie's Head,
John Case yet lives, though Saffold's dead.
                    JOHN CASE? (fl. 1680–1700)

214 Over Case's Door

Within this place
Lives Doctor Case.

(The above couplet is claimed by Addison to have made more
money for Case than all the works of Dryden made for their
author.)
                    JOHN CASE (fl. 1680–1700)

215 From One of Case's Pill-Boxes

Here's fourteen pills for thirteen pence;
Enough in any man's own conscience.
                    JOHN CASE (fl. 1680–1700)

216 Inscription for the Sign of 'The Jolly Barber', with a Razor in One Hand, and a Pot of Beer in the Other

Roam not from *pole* to *pole*, but enter here,
Where naught exceeds the *shaving*, but the *beer*.
                    JONATHAN SWIFT (1667–1745)

217 From a Tobacco Wrapper

At DRUGGER'S HEAD, without a puff,
You'll ever find the best of snuff,
   Believe me, I'm not joking;
Tobacco, too, of every kind,
The very best you'll always find,
   For chewing or for smoking.

Tho' Abel, when the Humour's in,
At Drury Lane to make you grin,
   May sometimes take his station;
At number Hundred-Forty-Six,
In Fenchurch Street he now does fix
   His present Habitation.

His best respects he therefore sends,
And thus acquaints his generous Friends,
   From Limehouse up to Holborn,
That his rare snuffs are sold by none.
Except in Fenchurch Street alone,
   And there by Peter Cockburn.
                ANON (18th century?)

218 *From* London Evening Post

Ye Beauties, Beaux, ye Pleaders at the Bar,
Wives, Husbands, lovers, every one beside,
Who'd have their heads deficient rectify'd,
The Dentist famed who by just application
Excels each other operator in the Nation,
In Coventry's known street, near Leicester Fields,
At the *Two Heads* full satisfaction yields.
Teeth artificial he fixes so secure,
That as our own they usefully endure;

[205]

Not merely outside show and ornament
But ev'ry property of Teeth intent;
To eat, as well as speak, and form support
The falling cheeks and stumps from further hurt.
Nor is he daunted when the whole is gone,
But by an art peculiar to him known,
He'll so supply, you'll think you've got your own.

ANON (mid-18th century)

219 From a Marriage Broker's Card, 1776

Ye Nymphs forlorn, who pine away in Shades!
Ye mournful Widows, wailing for—Brocades!
Coxcombs who sigh for—Mode! and sighing Wits!
Bucks of St. James's! and ye Half-moon'd Cits!
Ye old and young—the ugly and the fair!
To Hymen's Shrine haste, sacrifice despair.
Let Law divorce, tyrannic Husbands rail,
Hence dare their Ire!—for here's enough for sale.
Let Virtue's mask the Wife awhile pursue,
Here's fresh Supply—here Wives of ev'ry Hue!
Black, white, red, grey—the bright, the dull, the witty!
Here's Dames for Courtiers, misses for the City!

ANON

220 *From the* Caledonian Mercury

(Preceding a letter of thanks from a sailor written with his new artificial hands)

G. Wilson humbly as before
Resumes his thankfulness once more
By favours formerly enjoy'd
In, by the public, being employ'd.

And hopes this public intimation
Will meet with candid acceptation.
The world knows well he makes *boots* neatly
And, as times go, he sells them cheaply.
'Tis also known to many a hundred
Who at his late invention wonder'd,
That polish'd *leather boxes, cases,*
So well known now in many places,
With *powder-flasks* and *porter-mugs,*
And jointed *leather arms* and *legs.*
Design'd for use as well as show,
Exempli gratia read below,
Were his invention; and no claim
Is just by any other name.
With numbers of production more,
In leather ne'er performed before.
In these dead times being almost idle,
He tried and made a *leather fiddle.*
Of workmanship extremely neat,
Of tone quite true, both soft and sweet.
And finding leather not a mute,
He made a *leather German flute,*
Which play'd as well and was as good
As any ever made of wood.
He for an idle hour's amusement
Wrote this exotic advertisement,
Informing you he does reside
In head of Canongate, south side,
Up the first wooden-railed stair,
You're sure to find his Whimship there.
In Britain none can fit you better
Than can your servant the *Bootmaker.*

GAVIN WILSON (fl. 1779)
('Arm, Leg and Boot maker, *but not* to his
Royal Highness the Prince of Wales')

221 The Cat and the Boot; *Or*, an Improvement upon Mirrors*

As I one morning shaving sat,
    For dinner-time preparing,
A dreadful howling from the cat
    Set all the room a staring!
Suddenly I turn'd—beheld a scene
    I could not but delight in;
For in my boots, so bright and clean,
    The Cat her face was fighting.
Bright was the boot—its surface fair,
    In lustre nothing lacking;
I never saw one half so clear,
    Except by WARREN's *Blacking*.
(WARREN! that name shall last as long
    As beaux and belles shall dash on,
Immortalis'd in every song
    That chaunts the praise of fashion.
For oh! without his *Blacking*, all
    Attempts we may abolish
To raise upon our boots at all
    The least of jet or polish.)
Surpris'd, its brilliancy I view'd
    With silent admiration;
The glass that on the table stood
    Wax'd dimly in its station.
I took the Boot, the glass displac'd,
    For soon I was aware,
The latter only was disgrac'd
    Whene'er the Boot was near.
And quickly found that I could shave
    Much better by its bloom,
Than any mirror that I have
    Within my drawing-room.

*This advertisement was accompanied by a
famous George Cruikshank drawing of the
cat and boot.

[208]

And since that time, I've often smil'd
To think how puss was frighten'd
When at the Boot she tugg'd and toil'd,
By WARREN's *Blacking* brighten'd.
                    ANON (early 19th century)

222 An Auctioneer's Handbill

LYNN, 19th SEPTEMBER, 1810
First Tuesday in the next October,
Now do not doubt but we'll be sober!
If Providence permits us action,
You may depend upon
                    AN AUCTION,
                    At the stall
That's occupied by   WILLIAM HALL.

To enumerate a task would be—
The best way is to come and see;
But not to come too vague an errand,
We'll give a sketch which we will warrant.
    About *one hundred books*, in due lots,
And pretty near the same in *shoe-lasts*;
Coats, waistcoats, breeches, in shining *buttons*,
Perhaps ten thousand *leather cuttings*,
Sold at per pound—your lot but ask it,
Shall be weighed to you in a basket;
Some lot of *tools* to make a try on,
About one hundred-weight of *iron*;
Scales, earthenware, arm-chairs, a *tea-urn*,
Tea-chests, a *herring-tub*, and so on;
With various more that's our intention
Which are too tedious here to mention.
N.B.—To undeceive, 'fore you come nigher,
The duty charged upon the buyer;

[209]

And, should we find we're not perplext,
We'll keep it up the Tuesday next.

WILLIAM HALL (fl. 1810)

223 From a Printed Bill, Fixed in the Beak of One in a Group of Five Stuffed Owls in the Shop Window of a Bird Stuffer, at Richmond, Yorkshire

We five owls were once alive;
On birds and mice we used to thrive;
Through barns and towers oft did fly
In search of prey both wet and dry,
And on each shining summer's day
In hollow trees we pass'd our time away,
Till the cruel sportsman forc'd us to the field,
Then unto the gun we were obliged to yield;
But now we have undergone dissection,
To add and join this grand collection.
Glass eyes we have got and cannot see,
Spectacles are of use, but not to we;
Now no more birds or mice we pursue,
For we are stuff'd, and it is true,
By Mr. Stevenson, who stuff'd us five,
And hundreds more, as though they were alive.

W. STEVENSON
Stuffer of Birds, Animals, Reptiles, and Fish;
Dealer in Fishing-Tackle,
Richmond, Yorkshire.

ANON (c. 1820)

224 Goodman's Sauce

The goose that on our Ock's green shore
    Thrives to the size of Albatross,
Is twice the goose it was before,
    When washed with Neighbour Goodman's sauce.
And ye, fat eels and trout, may feed
    Where Kennet's silver waters toss,
Proud are your Berkshire hearts to bleed
    When drest with Goodman's prime Vale Sauce.

ANON (1840s)

225 From a Connecticut Newspaper

Julia, my wife, has grown quite rude;
She has left me in a lonesome mood;
She has left my board,
She has left my bed,
She has gave away my meat and bread,
She has left me in spite of friends and church,
She has carried with her all my shirts.
Now ye who read this paper,
Since she cut this reckless caper,
I will not pay one single fraction
For any debt of her contraction.

LEVI ROCKWELL
(East Windsor, Conn., 4 August 1853)

226 A Drinking Song

If ever your spirits are damp, low,
  And bilious; you should, I opine,
Just quaff a deep bumper of Lamplough—
  Of Lamplough's Pyretic Saline.

The title is quaint and eccentric—
  Is probably so by design—
But they say for disturbances ventric
  There's nought like Pyretic Saline.

Don't bid me become exegetic,
  Or tell me I'm only a scamp low,
If I can tell you more of Pyretic
  Saline manufactured by Lamplough.

ANON

From a mid-19th-century weekly

227 The Waverley Pen

They come as a boon and a blessing to men,
The Pickwick, the Owl, and the Waverley Pen.

ANON

228 Pain Paint

MY WIFE HAD AN ULCER
On her Leg
Thirteen years,
Caused by various veins
Extending from her ancle to her knee.
Some places eaten away
To the bone.

I have employed
Over twenty eminent physicians
At vast expense,
But all attempts at cure
Proved utterly abortive
Until I used Wolcott's Pain Paint,
Which the Doctors told me
Was humbug.
But humbug or not
It has done the work complete
In less than one month,
Removing the pain
At first application.
I kept her leg wet
With PAIN PAINT constantly
Till healed.
I wish we had more humbugs as useful
As Dr. Wolcott's PAIN PAINT.
I am well known in this city,
And any person
Can make further inquiry
At 101 West Street, New York,
At the Hanover House
Of which I am proprietor.
And I think I can satisfy
All as to the benefit
Derived by the use of PAIN PAINT.
                    PETER MINCK (12 May 1868)

229 Plantation Bitters

To be, or not to be, that is the question.
Whether to suffer with mental anguish,
Feverish lips, cracking pains, dyspeptic agonies,
And nameless bodily suffering;
Or whether, with sudden dash,

Seize a bottle of PLANTATION BITTERS,
And, as Gunther swears, be myself a man again.
Gunther said my eyes were sallow,
My visage haggard, my breath tremendous bad,
My disposition troublesome—in fact,
He gently hinted that I was fast becoming
Quite a nuisance.
Four bottles now beneath my vest have disappeared:
My food has relish, my appetite is keen,
My step elastic, my mind brilliant, and
Nine pounds avoirdupois is added to my weight.

ANON (late 19th century)
From Harper's Weekly

230 Saved

It was a chill November eve and on the busy town
A heavy cloud of yellow fog was sinking slowly down;
Upon the bridge of Waterloo, a prey to mad despair,
There stood a man with heavy brow, and deep-lined face
   of care.

One ling'ring look around he gave, he on the river cast
That sullen stare of rash resolve he meant should be his last.
Far down the old cathedral rose, a shadow grey and dim,
The light of day would dawn on that but ne'er again on him.

One plunge within the murky stream would end the bitter
   strife.
'What rests there now,' he sobbed aloud, 'to bid me cling
   to life?'
Just then the sound of stamping feet smote on his list'ning
   ear,
A sandwich-man upon his beat paused 'neath the lamplight
   clear.

One hurried glance—he read the board that hung upon his
   back,
He leapt down from the parapet, and smote his thigh a
   smack.
'I must see that,' he cried—the words that put his woe to
   flight
Were 'John S. Clark as Acres at the Charing Cross tonight.'

ANON
From a theatrical paper, 1870s

231 A Prize-Winning Limerick

(In 1907 a prize of £3 a week for life was offered for the best
final line to a promotional limerick. The result was published
in the *Westminster Gazette* on 23 October 1907. The winner was
a Mr R. Rhodes.)

That the Traylee's the best cigarette,
Is a 'tip' that we cannot forget.
   And in buying, I'll mention
   There's a three pound a week pension,
Two good 'lines'—one you give, one you get.
ANON and R. RHODES (fl. 1907)

232 Force

Jim Dumps was a most unfriendly man,
Who lived his life on the hermit plan.
In his gloomy way he'd gone through life
And made the most of woe and strife,
Till Force one day was served to him.
Since then they've called him Sunny Jim.
ANON (early 20th century)

[215]

233 From a London Bookshop

Holy Scripture, Writ Divine,
Leather bound, at one and nine,
Satan trembles when he sees
Bibles sold as cheap as these.

ANON (20th century)

234 Advertising Epitaphs

From Upton-on Severn, Gloucestershire

Beneath this stone, in hopes of Zion,
Doth lie the landlord of the Lion;
His son keeps on the business still,
Resigned unto the heavenly will.

On a Quack

I was a Quack, and there are men who say
That in my time I physicked men away,
And that at length I by myself was slain,
By my own doings ta'en to relieve my pain.
The truth is, being troubled with a cough,
I, like a fool, consulted Dr. Gough,
Who physicked to death at his own will,
Because he's licensed by the State to kill.
Had I but wisely taken my own physic
I never should have died of cold and 'tisick.
So all be warned, and when you catch a cold
Go to my son, by whom my medicine's sold.

[216]

On one Lockyer, inventor of a patent medicine (17th century)

Here Lockyer lyes interred, enough his Name
Speakes one hath few Competitors in Fame;
A Name so great, so gen'ral, it may scorn
Inscriptions, which do vulgar Tombs adorn;
His Vertues and his Pills are so well known,
That Envy can't confine them under Stone;
This Verse is lost, his PILL embalmes him safe
To future Times without an Epitaph.

235 The Advertising Agency Song

When your client's hopping mad,
Put his picture in the ad.
If he still should prove refractory
Add a picture of his factory.

ANON

236 A Ternarie of Littles, upon a Pipkin of Jellie
Sent to a Lady

1   A little Saint best fits a little Shrine,
      A little prop best fits a little Vine,
      As my small Cruse best fits my little Wine.

2   A little Seed best fits a little Soyle,
      A little Trade best fits a little Toyle:
      As my small Jarre best fits my little Oyle.

3   A little Bin best fits a little Bread,
      A little Garland fits a little Head:
      As my small stuffe best fits my little Shed.

4   A little Hearth best fits a little Fire,
      A little Chappel fits a little Quire,
      As my small Bell best fits my little Spire.

5   A little streame best fits a little Boat;
      A little lead best fits a little Float;
      As my small Pipe best fits my little note.

6   A little meat best fits a little bellie,
      As sweetly Lady, give me leave to tell ye,
      This little Pipkin fits this little Jellie.
                    ROBERT HERRICK (1591–1674)

237 The Primrose

Ask me why I send you here
This firstling of the infant year;
Ask me why I send to you
This primrose all bepearl'd with dew;
I straight will whisper in your ears,
The sweets of love are washed with tears;—
Ask me why this flower doth show
So yellow, green, and sickly too;
Ask me why the stalk is weak,
And bending, yet it doth not break;
I must tell you, these discover
What doubts and fears are in a lover.

THOMAS CAREW (1595–1640)

238 To a Young Lady, with Some Lampreys*

With lovers 'twas of old the fashion
By presents to convey their passion;
No matter what the gift they sent,
The lady saw that love was meant.
Fair Atlanta, as a favour,
Took the boar's head her hero gave her;
Nor could the bristly thing affront her;
'Twas a fit present from a hunter.
When squires send woodcocks to the dame,
It serves to show their absent flame.
Some by a snip of woven hair,
In posied lockets, bribe the fair.

*Believed to have aphrodisiac qualities.

[219]

How many mercenary matches
Have sprung from diamond-rings and watches!
But hold—a ring, a watch, a locket,
Would drain at once a poet's pocket;
He should send songs that cost him nought,
Nor ev'n be prodigal of thought.

 Why then send lampreys? Fie, for shame!
'Twill set a virgin's blood on flame.
This to fifteen a proper gift!
It might lend sixty-five a lift.

 I know your maiden aunt will scold,
And think my present somewhat bold.
I see her lift her hands and eyes:
'What; eat it, niece; eat Spanish flies!
Lamprey's a most immodest diet:
You'll neither wake nor sleep in quiet.
Should I tonight eat sago-cream,
'Twould make me blush to tell my dream:
If I eat lobster, 'tis so warming,
That every man I see looks charming.
Wherefore had not the filthy fellow
Laid Rochester upon thy pillow?
I vow and swear, I think the present
Had been as modest and as decent.

 'Who has her virtue in her power?
Each day has its unguarded hour,
Always in danger of undoing,
A prawn, a shrimp, may prove our ruin!

 'The shepherdess, who lives on sallad,
To cool her youth, controls her palate.
Should Dian's maids turn liquorish livers,
And of huge lampreys rob the rivers,
Then, all beside each glade and visto,
You'd see nymphs lying like Calisto.

 'The man, who meant to heat your blood,
Needs not himself such vicious food—'

 In this, I own, your aunt is clear,
I sent you what I well might spare:

For, when I see you, (without joking)
Your eyes, lips, breasts, are so provoking,
They set my heart more cock-a-hoop,
Than could whole seas of crawfish soup.

JOHN GAY (1685–1732)

239 To Miss Lucy F——, with a New Watch

With me while present, may thy lovely eyes
    Be never turn'd upon this golden toy:
Think ev'ry pleasing hour too swiftly flies,
    And measure time, by joy succeeding joy.

But when the cares that interrupt our bliss
    To me not always will thy sight allow,
Then oft with kind impatience look on this,
    Then every minute count—as I do now.

GEORGE LYTTELTON (1709–73)

240 Sent to Miss Bell H——, with a Pair of Buckles

Happy trifles, can ye bear
Sighs of fondness to the fair;
If your pointed tongues can tell,
How I love my charming Bell?
Fondly take a lover's part,
Plead the anguish of my heart.
  Go—ye trifles—gladly fly,
(Gracious in my fair-one's eye)
Fly—your envy'd bliss to meet;
Fly, and kiss the charmer's feet.

[221]

Happy there, with waggish play,
Though you revel day by day,
Like the donor, ev'ry night,
(Robb'd of his supreme delight)
To subdue your wanton pride,
Useless, you'll be thrown aside.

JOHN CUNNINGHAM (1729–73)

241 Sent to a Lady, with a Seal

Th'impression which this seal shall make,
The rougher hand of force may break;
Or jealous Time, with slow decay,
May all its traces wear away;
But neither time nor force combin'd,
Shall tear thy image from my mind;
Nor shall the sweet *impression* fade
Which Chloe's thousand charms have made;
For spite of time, or force, or art,
'Tis *seal'd* for ever on my heart.

ROBERT LLOYD (1733–64)

242 Sent to a Patient, with the Present of a Couple of Ducks

I've dispatch'd, my dear madam, this scrap of a letter,
To say that Miss ——— is very much better.
A Regular Doctor no longer she lacks,
And therefore I've sent her a couple of Quacks.

DR EDWARD JENNER (1749–1823)

243 Stanzas to a Lady, with the Poems of Camoëns

This votive pledge of fond esteem,
　　Perhaps, dear girl! for me thou'lt prize;
It sings of Love's enchanting dream,
　　A theme we never can despise.

Who blames it but the envious fool,
　　The old and disappointed maid;
Or pupil of the prudish school,
　　In single sorrow doom'd to fade?

Then read, dear girl! with feeling read,
　　For thou wilt ne'er be one of those;
To thee in vain I shall not plead
　　In pity for the poet's woes.

He was in sooth a genuine bard;
　　His was no faint, fictitious flame.
Like his, may love be thy reward,
　　But not thy hapless fate the same.

GEORGE GORDON, LORD BYRON
(1788–1824)

244 With a China Chamberpot, to the Countess of Hillsborough

Too proud, too delicate to tell her wants
Her lover guesses them, and gladly grants;
The wish that he still trembles to explain
She long has known but bids him wish in vain;
With tears incessant he laments his case,
And can have small occasion for this vase.

Go then beneath her bed or toilet stand,
But chiefly after tea be near at hand;
Sure of her notice then, then take your fill,
Nor fear one drop her tidy hand should spill,
Though Cyder or Champagne supply the source,
And laughter hurry forth the rapid course.
Who talks of the Pierian spring or stream?
But stop dear Muse, lest on th'enchanting theme
My warm imagination should proceed
To what you must not write, she must not read.
                              Kings-gate, 1764.
        HENRY FOX, LORD HOLLAND (1705–74)

245 To a Lady, with a Compass

The *needle* quivering from its pole,
    Drawn by each worthless nail,
Is a true emblem of the soul,
    When passion's powers prevail:

Plung'd in attractive pleasure's course,
    It fondly sweeps along;
But touch'd with virtue's magnet force,
    It trembles doing wrong.
    THE HON. GEORGE NAPIER (1751–1804)
    From *Asylum for Fugitive Pieces*, 1799

246 To a Lady, with a Present of a Fan

Smiling, sweet girl, this proffer'd toy approve,
Cool tho'its use, the gift of warmest love.
    Prest by thy genial hand, behold it spread,
In pride expansive, its elastic head;

(For thy dear fingers sensitive caress,
Instant can raise it, instantly depress);
Then, betwixt polish'd shafts of equal size,
From the round-swelling centre stately rise;
'Till, in full lustre, all its beauties play,
Like rose-buds opening to the vernal ray:
For to the circulating orb below,
Solely its captivating powers we owe;
Powers, which to pleasure every joint constrain,
Till to its shape relax it shrinks again.
  Its winning graces and seducing air,
Engage the wife, and prepossess the fair;
Ev'n virgin modesty, exempt from harms,
May oft employ its inoffensive charms;
For of its use no mark it leaves, no stain,
Can from so pure an effluence remain.
For where's that lynx's piercing eye can trace
The track of eagles through th'aethereal space?
The serpent's devious maze along the plain?
Ship's paths – or winds that ventilate the main?
  The brunette widow too may find relief
From this, to mitigate her ardent grief,
May to her wish this pliant engine frame,
To cool her passions, or to fan their flame.

CHARLES BRANDLING (1733–1802)
From *Asylum for Fugitive Pieces*, 1799

247 To Lydia, with a Coloured Egg, on Easter Monday

In Scotia so fair, 'tis a custom they say,
  Old Time hath brought down with his stream,
Each friend to present with an egg on this day,
  As a token of love or esteem.

But why or wherefore, is a matter, I wot,
 Tradition withholds from my view,
And since the original cause I have not,
 I'll brood over this for one new.

It bears, my dear Lyd, when minutely defined,
 A fanciful semblance of thee,
Thy heart is its centre, its white is thy mind,
 It shell and thine honour agree.

If once, from neglect, an egg falls to the ground,
 No art can its virtue restore;
If once at its post honour's not to be found,
 We look there for honour no more.

Since honour's defection will virtue expose,
 And bliss with its purity dwells,
The treasure within thy fair bosom enclose,
 As eggs are enclosed in their shells.

JOHN JONES (1774–?)
From *Attempts in Verse*
'by John Jones, an old servant', 1831

248   To a Lady,* with a Present of a Walking-Stick

A compliment upon a crutch
Does not appear to promise much;
A theme no lover ever chose
For writing billet-doux in prose,
Or for an amatory sonnet;
But this I may comment upon it.

*Jemima, Dowager Countess of Errol, whom Frere later married.

Its heart is whole, its head is light;
'Tis smooth and yielding, yet upright.
In this you see an emblem of the donor,
Clear and unblemish'd as his honour;
Form'd for your use, framed to your hand,
Obedient to your last command.
Its proper place is by your side,
Its main utility and pride
To be your prop, support, and guide.

JOHN HOOKHAM FRERE (1769–1846)

249 A Feather's Weight

(With the present of a quill pen)

'The pen is mightier than the sword;'
Yes; and a woman's lightest word
Is sometimes more to hapless men
Than stroke of sword or thrust of pen.

No word is lighter than this holder—
A feather's weight; but I, grown older
Than once I was, remember still
How men do trust to women's will
As to the turning of a feather—
Her 'Yes' or 'No', and 'Wonder whether. . .?'
Some pity, therefore, moves me now
For that most wise and fortunate Other,
That future-coming man and brother
Whose heart shall wait to hear your vow.
Be sure that, when his whole fate lingers
On pen-tip 'twixt those gentle fingers,
Not for a single fault you slay him,
But in all features duly weigh him.

[227]

This painted quill itself's the measure
Of what should be your queenly pleasure;
For, in awards of bliss or bale,
A feather often turns the scale.

G. P. LATHROP
From *Harper's New Monthly Magazine*, 1882

250 To——, with an Ivory Hand-Glass

Look in this crystal pool, and you will see
(Haloed in gold, enshrined in ivory)
What Heaven's unopened windows hid from me.

Whence this enchantment, weaving spells that bind
With sightless cords my visionary mind?
What angel, dark or shining, lurks behind?

Eyes of the flesh still blind, unfolded scroll
Hiding its mystery! God knows the whole.
I guess your face the shadow of your soul.

LORD ALFRED DOUGLAS (1870–1945)

251 Useful for Book-Plates

Who folds a leafe downe
Ye divel toaste browne;
Who makes marke or blotte
Ye divel roaste hot;
Who stealeth thise boke
Ye divel shall cooke.

ANON

To his booke

Who with thy leaves shall wipe (at need)
The place, where swelling *Piles* do breed:
May every ill, that bites, or smarts,
Perplexe him in his hinder-parts.

ROBERT HERRICK (1591–1674)

Hic liber ad me pertinet
To keep it well in mind
Ad me Robertum Barclay
Most courteous and kind.
Si aliquis invenerit
Gar him gie it again
Non illam preciptorum
Shal gar get his ain.

ROBERT BARCLAY (1699–1760)

Here do I put my name for to betraye
The thief yᵗ steals my book away.

ANON (dated 1723)

[229]

John Smith is my name,
England is my nation,
London is my dwelling place,
And Christ is my salvation.
And when I'm dead and in my grave,
And all my bones are rotten,
When this you see, remember me,
Though I am long forgotten.

ANON

252 Seven Items from the Scrapbooks of E. Wilson Dobbs

This book is mine
By right divine;
And if it go astray,
I'll call you kind
My desk to find
And put it safe away.

ANON

Whoe'er this book, if lost, doth find,
I hope will have a generous mind,
And bring it to the owner—me,
Whose name they'll see page fifty-three.

ANON

Steal not this book for fear of shame,
For in it is the owner's name;
And when you die the Lord will say,
'Where is that book you stole away?'

[230]

Then, if you say you do not know,
The Lord will say, 'Go down below';
But if you say you cannot tell,
The Lord will say, 'Oh, go to h——.'

ANON

To the borrower of this book

Hic liber est meus,
Deny it who can,
Samuel Showell, Jr.
An honest man.
In vico corvino (locale appended)
I am to be found,
Si non mortuus sum,
And laid in the ground.
At si non vivens,
You will find an heir
Qui librum recipiet:
You need not to fear.
Ergo cum lectus est
Restore it, and then
Ut quando mutuaris
I may lend it again.
At si detineas,
So let it be lost
Expectabo Argentum
As much as it cost (viz. 5s.).

SAMUEL SHOWELL, JR.

From a copy of the *Companion to
the Festivals and Fasts*, 1717

Neither blemish this book, nor the leaves double down,
Nor lend it to each idle friend in the town;
Return it when read; or, if lost, please supply
Another as good to the mind and the eye.
With right and with reason you need but be friends
And each book in my study your pleasure attends.

ANON

This book is one thing,
My fist is another;
Touch this one thing,
You'll sure feel the other.

ANON

This is Thomas Jones's book—
You may just within it look;
But you'd better do no more,
For the Devil's at the door,
And will snatch at fingering hands;
Look behind you—there he stands!

THOMAS JONES?

All seven items were printed in
Notes and Queries, 1899

253 Lines Written in the Front of a Well-Read Copy of Burns's *Songs*

To the reader

Afore ye tak in hand this beuk
To these few lines jist gie a leuk.

Be sure that baith ye'r hands are clean,
Sic as are fitten to be seen,

[232]

Free fra a' dirt, an' black coal coom;
Fra ash-hole dust, an' chimley bloom;
O' creesh fra candle or fra lamp,
Upon it leave naè filthy stamp.
I'd rather gie a siller croon,
Than see a butter'd finger'd loon,
Wi' parritch, reemin fra his chaps,
Fast fa'in down in slav'rin draps
Upon the beuk. Hech! for each sowp,
I'd wish a nettle in his doup;
For every creeshie drap transparent,
I'd wish his neck wi' a sair hair in't:
Sic plague spots on ilk bonnie page,
Wad mak a sant e'en stamp wi' rage.
    Reader, ye'll no tak amiss,
Sic an impertinence as this:
Ye'r no the ane that e'er wad do't—
An use a beuk like an old cloot;
Ye wadna wi' y'er fingers soil it—
Nor creesh, nor blot, not rend, nor spoil it.

ANON

Printed in Leigh Hunt's London Journal,
no. 34, 19 November 1834

254 Book-Lender's Lament

I of my Spenser quite bereft,
Last Winter sore was shaken;
Of Lamb I've but a quarter left,
Nor could I save my Bacon.

They pick'd my Locke, to me far more
Than Bramah's patent worth,
And now my losses I deplore
Without a Home on earth.

They still have made me slight returns,
And thus my grief divide;
For, oh! they've cured me of my Burns,
And eased my Akenside.

But all I think I shall not say,
Nor let my anger burn,
For as they have not found me Gay,
They have not left me Sterne.

ANON

23 Useful for Correspondence

255 A True and Faithful Inventory of the Goods Belonging to Dr Swift, Vicar of Laracor; upon Lending His House to the Bishop of Meath, Till His Palace was Rebuilt

An oaken, broken elbow-chair;
A cawdle-cup, without an ear;
A batter'd, shatter'd ash bedstead;
A box of deal, without a lid;
A pair of tongs, but out of joint;
A back-sword poker, without point;
A pot that's crack'd across, around
With an old knotted garter bound;
An iron lock, without a key;
A wig, with hanging quite grown grey;
A curtain worn to half a stripe;
A pair of bellows, without pipe;
A dish which might good meat afford once;
An Ovid, and an old Concordance;
A bottle-bottom, wooden platter,
One is for meal, and one for water:
There likewise is a copper skillet,
Which runs as fast out as you fill it;
A candlestick, snuff-dish, and save-all:
And thus your household goods you have all.
These to your lordship as a friend,
Till you have built, I freely lend:
They'll serve your lordship for a shift;
Why not, as well as doctor Swift?

JONATHAN SWIFT (1667–1745)

256 Tax Return

The following curious Return has lately been sent in to the Commissioners for the Income Tax, the veracity of which may be depended upon:

> I, —— A.B. do declare
> I have but little money to spare.
> > I have,
> > 1 Little house.
> > 1 Little maid.
> > 2 Little boys.
> > 2 Little trade.
> > 2 Little land
> > 2 Ditto money at command.
> Rather too little is my little all
> To supply with comfort my dear little squall,
> And 2 too little to pay Taxes at all.
> > By this you see
> > I have children three
> > Depend on me.
> > > ANON (*Shrewsbury Chronicle*)
> > > From *A Cabinet of Curiosities*,
> > > Joseph Taylor, 1807

257 The Inventory, in Answer to the Usual Mandate Sent by a Surveyor of the Taxes, Requiring a Return of the Number of Horses, Servants, Carriages, etc. Kept

> Sir, as your mandate did request,
> I send you here a faithfu' list
> O' gudes an' gear, an' a' my graith,
> To which I'm clear to gi'e my aith.

[236]

Imprimis then, for carriage cattle,
I have four brutes o' gallant mettle,
As ever drew before a pettle;
My han' afore's a gude auld has-been,
An' wight an' wilfu' a' his days been;
My han' ahin's a weel gaun fillie,
That aft has borne me hame frae Killie,
An' your auld burrough mony a time,
In days when riding was nae crime—
But ance whan in my wooing pride
I like a blockhead boost to ride,
The wilfu' creature sae I pat to,
(Lord, pardon a' my sins an' that too!)
I play'd my fillie sic a shavie,
She's a' bedevil'd wi' the spavie.
My furr-ahin's a wordy beast,
As e'er in tug or tow was trac'd.
The fourth's, a Highland Donald hastie,
A damn'd red-wud Kilburnie blastie.
Foreby a Cowte, o' Cowte's the wale,
As ever ran afore a tail;
If he be spar'd to be a beast,
He'll draw me fifteen pun at least.

Wheel carriages I ha'e but few,
Three carts, an' twa are feckly new;
An auld wheel barrow, mair for token,
Ae leg, an' baith the trams, are broken;
I made a poker o' the spin'le,
An' my auld mother burnt the trin'le.

For men, I've three mischievous boys,
Run de'ils for rantin' an' for noise;
A gaudsman ane, a thrasher t'other,
Wee Davock hauds the nowte in fother.
I rule them as I ought discreetly,
An' often labour them completely.
An' aye on Sundays duly nightly,
I on the questions tairge them tightly;
Till faith, wee Davock's grown sae gleg,
Tho' scarcely langer than my leg

He'll screed you aff Effectual Calling,
As fast as ony in the dwalling.
    I've nane in female servan' station,
(Lord keep me aye frae a' temptation!)
I ha'e nae wife, and that my bliss is,
An' ye have laid nae tax on misses;
An' then if kirk folks dinna clutch me,
I ken the devils dare na touch me.
Wi' weans I'm mair than weel contented,
Heav'n sent me ane mae than I wanted.
My sonsie smirking dear-bought Bess,
She stares the daddy in her face,
Enough of ought ye like but grace.
But her, my bonnie sweet wee lady,
I've paid enough for her already.
An' gin ye tax her or her mither,
B' the Lord, ye'se get them a' thegither.
    And now, remember, Mr. Aiken,
Nae kind of license out I'm takin';
Frae this time forth, I do declare,
I'se ne'er ride horse nor hizzie mair;
Thro' dirt and dub for life I'll paidle,
Ere I sae dear pay for a saddle;
My travel a' on foot I'll shank it,
I've sturdy bearers, Gude be thankit!
The Kirk an' you may tak' you that,
It puts but little in your pat;
Sae dinna put me in your buke,
Nor for my ten white shillings luke.
    This list wi' my ain han' I wrote it,
The day an' date as under notit:
Then know all ye whom it concerns,
Subscripsi huic—ROBERT BURNS.
                    Mossgiel, February 22, 1786.
                    ROBERT BURNS (1759–96)

258 Extraordinary Will

Mr. Jackett, one of the principal clerks belonging to Messrs. Fuller and Co. died suddenly at the Royal Exchange, in the Year 1789, and left the following Will, which was proved in Doctor's Commons:

I give and bequeath
(When I'm laid underneath)
To my two loving sisters most dear,
The whole of my store,
(Were it twice as much more,)
Which God's goodness has granted me here.
And that none may prevent
This my will and intent,
Or occasion the least of law racket;
With a solemn appeal,
I confirm, sign, and seal,
This, the true act and deed of
WILL JACKETT (?–1789)
From *Cabinet of Curiosities*, Joseph Taylor, 1807

259 A Letter from School

Written at the age of nine

Dear Mother, I attempt to write you a letter
In verse—tho' in prose, I could do it much better:
The Muse this cold weather sleeps up at Parnassus,
And leaves us, poor poets, as stupid as asses.
She'll tarry still longer, if she has a warm chamber,
A store of old Massic, Ambrosia, and Amber.
Dear Mother, don't laugh, you may think she is tipsy,
And I, if a poet, must drink like a gipsy . . .
All the boys at our school, are well, tho', yet, many
Are suffer'd at home, to suck eggs with their Granny.

'To-morrow,' says daddy, 'you must go my dear Billy,
To Englefield House; do not cry, you are silly.'
Says the Mother, all dress'd in silk, and in sattin;
'Don't cram the poor boy, with your Greek, and your
    Latin;
I'll have him a little longer, before mine own eyes;
To nurse him, and feed him, with tarts, and minc'd pies;
We'll send him to school, when the weather is warmer:
Come, kiss me, my pretty, my sweet little charmer.'

But now I must banish all fun, and all folly;
So doleful's the news, I am going to tell ye:
Poor Wade! my schoolfellow, lies low in the gravel;
One month ere fifteen, put an end to his travel:
Harmless, and mild, and remark'd for goodnature:
The cause of his death was his overgrown stature:
His epitaph I wrote, as inserted below;
What tribute more friendly, could I on him bestow.
The bard craves one shilling, of his own dear Mother;
And if you think proper, add to it another.

Epitaph

Here lies interr'd, in silent shade,
The frail remains of Hamlet Wade;
A youth more prom'sing, ne'er took breath;
But ere fifteen, laid cold in death!
Ye young! ye old! and ye of middle age!
Act well your part, for quit the stage
Of mortal life one day you must;
And like him moulder into dust.
                    THOMAS LOVE PEACOCK (1785–1866)

260 Reply to a Creditor

(Written three hours before the author's death in 1816, in response to an application for payment of a small debt, addressed to Judge Harding, 'if living, or to his executors, if dead'.)

Dear Messrs. Tippins, what is feared by you,
Alas! the melancholy circumstance is true,
That I am *dead*! And more afflicting still,
My legal assets *cannot pay your bill!*
To think of this I'm almost broken-hearted—
Insolvent I this earthly life departed!
Dear Messrs. T., I'm yours without a farthing.
For *executors* and self,

GEORGE HARDING (?–1816)

261 Epistle to Mr. Murray

My dear Mr. Murray,
You're in a damn'd hurry,
  To set up this ultimate Canto;
But (if they don't rob us)
You'll see Mr. Hobhouse
  Will bring it safe in his portmanteau.

For the Journal you hint of,
As ready to print off,
  No doubt you do right to commend it;
But as yet I have writ off
The devil a bit of
  Our 'Beppo:'—when copied, I'll send it.

Then you've . . .'s Tour,—
No great things, to be sure,—
  You could hardly begin with a less work;

[241]

For the pompous rascallion,
Who don't speak Italian
  Nor French, must have scribbled by guess work.

You can make any loss up
With 'Spence' and his gossip,
  A work which must surely succeed;
Then Queen Mary's Epistle-craft,
With the new 'Fytte' of 'Whistlecraft,'
  Must make people purchase and read.

Then you've General Gordon,
Who girded his sword on,
  To serve with a Muscovite master
And help him to polish
A nation so owlish,
  They thought shaving their beards a disaster.

For the man, 'poor and shrewd,'
With whom you'd conclude
  A compact without more delay,
Perhaps some such pen is
Still extant in Venice;
  But please, sir, to mention *your pay*.

                Venice, January 8, 1818.
    GEORGE GORDON, LORD BYRON (1788–1824)

262 To Alfred Tennyson

I entreat you, Alfred Tennyson,
Come and share my haunch of venison.
I have too a bin of claret,
Good, but better when you share it.
Though 'tis only a small bin,
There's a stock of it within.

And as sure as I'm a rhymer
Half a butt of Rudesheimer.
Come: among the sons of men is one
Welcomer than Alfred Tennyson?
WALTER SAVAGE LANDOR (1775–1865)

263 Lines Left at Mr. Theodore Hook's House in June, 1834

As Dick and I
Were a-sailing by
At Fulham bridge, I cock'd my eye,
And says I, 'Add-zooks!
There's Theodore Hook's,
Whose Sayings and Doings make such pretty books.

'I wonder,' says I,
Still keeping my eye
On the house, 'if he's in—I should like to try;'
With his oar on his knee,
Says Dick, says he,
'Father, suppose you land and see!'

'What land and *sea*,'
Says I to he,
'Together! why Dick, why how can that be?'
And my comical son,
Who is fond of fun,
I thought would have split his sides at the pun.

So we rows to shore,
And knocks at the door—
When William, a man I've seen often before,
Makes answer and says,
'Master's gone in a chaise
Call'd a *homnibus*, drawn by a couple of bays.'

[243]

So I says then,
'Just lend me a pen:'
'I will, sir,' says William, politest of men;
So having no card, these poetical brayings,
Are the record I leave of my doings and sayings.
RICHARD H. BARHAM (1788–1845)

264 Memorial Verses for Travellers

Purse, dirk, cloak, night-cap, kerchief, shoeing-horn,
  buget,* and shoes;
Spear, nails, hood, halter, sadle-cloth, spurs, hat, withy
  horse-comb:
Bow, arrow, sword, buckler, horn, brush, gloves, string,
  and thy bracer;
Pen, paper, ink, parchment, red-wax, poms,† books, then
  remember;
Penknife, comb, thimble, needle, thread, point, lest that
  thy girth break;
Bodkin, knife, lingel,‡ give thy horse meat: see he be
  stowed well;
Make merry, sing an thou canst, take heed to thy geer, that
  thou lose none.

                    SIR ANTHONY FITZHERBERT (1470–1538)
                                      From *Husbandry*

265 Verses to be Repeated by an Attorney Leaving His Lodging to Wait upon Judges Riding the Circuits from One County to Another, Least He Forget Some Necessary Thing

Pen-knife, Quills, Ink-horn, Books, Paper, Table-Books,
  Caps; Take
Wax, Seal and Slippers, Sword, Knife and Dagger, safe
  make

*budget †pomanders ‡awl

Purse, Handkerchiefs, Shirts, Rings, Coat, and for your
    own sake,
Comb, Garters, Stockins, Gloves.

JOHN WILLIS (?–1628)
From *Mnemonica*

266 The Age of Animals

Thrice the age of a dog is that of a horse;
Thrice the age of a horse is that of a man;
Thrice the age of a man is that of a deer;
Thrice the age of a deer is that of an eagle.

ANON (Celtic rhyme)

267 How to Choose a Horse

One white foot, run him for your life;
Two white feet, keep him for your wife;
Three white feet, keep him for your man;
Four white feet, sell him if you can;
Four white feet and a stripe on the nose,
Knock him on the head and feed him to the crows.

ANON

268 How to Catch Trout

The rod light and taper, thy tackle fine,
    Thy lead ten inches upon the line;
Bigger or lesse, according to the stream,
    Angle in the dark, when others dream:

[246]

Or in a cloudy day with a lively worm,
  The Bradlin is best; but give him a turn
Before thou do land a large wel grown Trout.
  And if with a flye thou wilt have a bout,
Overload not with links, that the flye may fall
  First on the stream for that's all in all.
The line shorter than the rod, with a naturall flye:
  But the chief point of all is the cookery.

THOMAS BARKER (fl. 1651)

269 Baits for Various Fish

Late in the evening the ale graines and blood,
  Being well mixt together is bait very good
For Carp, Tench and Roch, and Dace to prepare,
  If early in the morning at the river you are.
Strong tackle for Carp; for Roch and Dace fine,
  Will help thee with fish sufficient to dine.
For the Carp let thy bait the knotted worm be,
  The rest love the cadice, the paste and the flye.

★ ★ ★

A live and small minnow is the best bait
  To kill a great Pearch by Anglers deceit,
A black snaile is the bait for the bonny Chub,
  A Barbell souced is meat very good.
The greedy Gudgeon doth love the Gild tail,
  And the twelve yard line doth never faile.
To kill of good Eeles an excellent dish,
  With nooses and baits of the little fish;
At the but of the oak take you the flye,
  And kill the Grayling immediately.
But when of all sorts thou hast thy wish,
  Follow *Barker's* advice to cook the fish.

THOMAS BARKER (fl. 1651)
268 and 269 from The Art of Angling

270 The Spelling of Elliot

Double L and single T,
Elliots of Minto and Wolflee.
Double T and single L,
The Eliotts they in Stobs that dwell.
Single L and Single T,
Eliots of St. Germains be.
But double L and Double T,
The de'il may ken wha *they* may be.

ANON

Printed in the preface to Highways
and Byways in the Border,
Andrew and James Lang, 1914

271 First Lessons in Musical Time

The Dowager Semibreve sat by the fire,
In as dignified state as her heart could desire;
Her matronly daughters, the Minims, sat near,
While their lively young progeny round them appear.

Of these four young Crotchets who marched in a row
Thought their Mother and Grandmother both very slow,
While laughing and playing and making a rout
Eight mad little Quavers came frisking about.

But language would fail in describing the din
When the Semys and Demys came frolicking in;
I thought for their mirth the old ladies would chide them,
So I managed to put up some bars to divide them.

But they, little caring for ought they might say,
On a ledger-line ladder got out of the way;
And some had two ticks, and some four, to their share,
While those who had dots were the merriest there.

[248]

I know not how long the gay dance might have lasted,
With the semibreve's gravity strangely contrasted,
When a stupid old Rest who was voted a dunce,
Came suddenly on them and stopped them at once.

ANON

272 A Rule for Shooting

Never, never let your gun
Pointed be at anyone.
All the pheasants ever bred
Won't make up for one man dead.

ANON

273 Useful for Avoiding Collisions at Sea

*(Rhymes based on the PORT/RED and
STARBOARD/GREEN lights carried by ships)*

When both lights you see ahead,
STARBOARD wheel and show your RED.

GREEN to GREEN or RED to RED—
Perfect safety, go ahead.

If to your STARBOARD RED appear,
'Tis your duty to keep clear;
To act as judgement says is proper—
To PORT or STARBOARD, back, or stop 'er.
But when upon your PORT is seen
A steamer's STARBOARD light of GREEN,
There's not so much for you to do,
for GREEN to PORT keeps clear of you.

[249]

Both in safety and in doubt,
Always keep a good look-out.
In danger with no room to turn,
Ease her, stop her, go astern.

ANON

274 The Rule of the Road

The rule of the road's an anomaly quite.
In riding or driving along:
If you go to the left, you are sure to go right,
If you go to the right, you are wrong.

ANON

25 Useful for All Circumstances

275 Sound Advice

When in danger or in doubt,
Run in circles, scream and shout.
                              ANON

Acknowledgements

For permission to reprint copyright material, the following acknowledgements are made:

For lines by Hilaire Belloc, from *Cautionary Verses*, published by Alfred A. Knopf, Inc., to Gerald Duckworth & Co., Ltd., and Alfred Knopf, Inc.—*Henry King; Franklin Hyde*.

For lines by Willard R. Espy: Reprinted from *The Game of Words* by Willard R. Espy. Copyright © MCMLXXI, MCMLXXII by Willard R. Espy. By permission of Bramhall House, a division of Clarkson N. Potter, Inc.—*Gemini Jones, Singular Singulars, Peculiar Plurals*.

For lines by Michael Flanders, from the show *At the Drop of Another Hat*, Copyright © The Estate of Michael Flanders.—*First and Second Law*.

*For lines by Lord Alfred Douglas, from *Lyrics*, published by Messrs Rich & Cowan.—*To ——, with an Ivory Hand Glass*.

For lines by A. P. Herbert, from *What A Word!*, published by Messrs Methuen & Co., Ltd., to A. P. Watt, Ltd. and Lady Gwendolyn Herbert.—*Inst., Ult. and Prox.*

For lines by Benjamin Hall Kennedy, from *The Revised Latin Primer*, to the Longman Group, Ltd.—*Memorial Lines on the Gender of Latin Substantives, List of Prepositions*.

For lines by Tom Lehrer:
For *The Elements*: © 1959 Tom Lehrer. Used by permission.
For *New Maths*: © 1965 Tom Lehrer. Used by permission.

For lines by Donald Monat, from *Salome Dear, Not In the Fridge*, edited by Arthur Marshall, To Messrs George Allen & Unwin.—*Mnemonic*.

For lines by Ogden Nash, from *Family Reunion*, by permission of the Estate of Ogden Nash, J. M. Dent & Sons, Ltd and Little, Brown & Company. *Reflection on Babies*: Copyright

---

*While every effort has been made to secure permission, it has in a few cases proved impossible to trace the author or his executor. We apologize for our apparent negligence.

1940 by Ogden Nash. *Lines to be Embroidered on A Bib, or, The Child is Father of the Man, But Not For Quite a While*: Copyright 1947 by Ogden Nash. First appeared in *The New Yorker*. *The Perfect Husband*: Copyright 1949 by Ogden Nash. *Celery*: Copyright 1941 by the Curtis Publishing Company. First appeared in the *Saturday Evening Post*.

For lines by Dorothy Parker, from *The Collected Dorothy Parker* and *The Portable Dorothy Parker*, reprinted by permission of Messrs Gerald Duckworth & Co., Ltd. and Viking Penguin Inc. Copyright 1926, copyright renewed 1954 by Dorothy Parker. — *Social Note, Unfortunate Coincidence, News Item*.

For lines by Gordon Perry, to the author. — *Aids for Latin, The Great Lakes of Canada*.

For lines by Justin Richardson, to the proprietors of *Punch*. — *Rhyme for Remembering How Many Nights there are in the Month, Rhyme for Remembering the Date of Easter*.